The HEART of Stable Relationships

12 ways The Healing Power of Horses can Transform Your Life

WENDY FELICITY FIRMIN-PRICE

All content is for information only and is not warranted for content accuracy or any other implied or explicit purpose.

Beautiful Cover Photographs by Emma Hughes of Horse Photography UK Surrey

Book cover design by Mohamed

First edition published by Wendy Felicity Firmin-Price

www.theheartofstablerelationships.com

Copyright © 2015

Wendy Felicity Firmin-Price has asserted her right under the Copyright, Designs, and Patents Act, 1988 to be identified as the author of this work.

ISBN 13: 978-1514616550
ISBN-10: 1514616556

I dedicate this book to my wonderful husband John and all of my horses

For showing me what unconditional love and giving is

I especially dedicate this to Tiggy my first pony who saved my life.

Thank you teaching me the heart of stable relationships.

Acknowledgements

I WOULD LIKE TO ACKNOWLEDGE AND thank:
   All of my horses past, present and future for without you there would be no point in getting up each day. Thank you for all your eternal optimism, patience and wisdom.

   My husband John, for giving me the freedom to get my book finished and always supporting me. Thank you for helping me get my life's work out to the world.

   All of my clients, past, present and future, especially my case study people in this book.

   Sam Blighe, my book editor, for her patience and professional touch to my book.

   Cynthia Platt my proof reader for her meticulous scrutiny and years of constant support and love.

   Christine King, my metaphysical guru, teacher and principal of the Metaphysical Society for the Expansion of Consciousness. Thank you for all your years of wisdom and support.

   For my numerous spiritual teachers especially Chuck Spezzano, Louise Hay, Robert Holden and Neil Donald Walsh, Joel Goldsmith, Ernest Holmes and Kevin.

   Vishal Morjaria my personal book architect for bringing it all together.

   Raymond Aaron, my publisher and New York Times

bestselling Author and Founder of the 10-10-10 amazing book mentoring programme.

All of my coaches, especially Kate Gerry, Peter Thomson.

My very special friend and mentor Elaine Wilkins.

Monica Andreéwitch and James French who are horse trainers extraordinaire.

All of my students, volunteers and especially Becky Wake for her endless hours of admin and support.

All of my staff for doing such a great job taking care of the yard, horses and me.

All of my past partners, especially for giving me the research into relationships.

All of my friends for continuing to believe in me.

Jackie Davis of Strides to Success for all her support, set up, mileage to & from The HEART Centre.

To all my holistic healers, therapists and body-workers for taking care of the horses well being.

All of my readers: I look forward to meeting some of you at our workshops.

Anyone I should have remembered and acknowledged, thank you.

Above all – The Infinite Intelligence of Life for inspiring the work through me.

> **"It is not I that have done the work,
> but the Infinite Power within"**

Foreword

I HAVE READ MANY BOOKS ON relationships. This book is very different. Throughout The Heart of Stable Relationships, Wendy Felicity Firmin-Price gives you amazing inspiration and insight about yourself and the people in your life, through the healing power of horses.

The varied real life stories about how the different ways Wendy's horses have transformed the lives and relationships of many humans is both fascinating and challenging to your own thinking, beliefs and behaviour.

I was very touched how Wendy shares her own personal challenging journey in a way that is very honest and captivating.

On reading the book you are compelled to want to experience for yourself how the healing power of horses can transform your life. I urge you to take advantage of the bonuses and offers throughout the book.

Raymond Aaron
New York Times Bestselling Author

Note To The Reader

THE INFORMATION, INCLUDING OPINION AND analysis, contained herein is based on the author's personal experiences and is not intended to provide professional advice.

The author and the publisher make no warranties, either expressed or implied, concerning the accuracy, applicability, effectiveness, reliability or suitability of the contents. If you wish to apply or follow the advice or recommendations mentioned herein, you take full responsibility for your actions. The author and publisher of this book shall in no event be held liable for any direct, indirect, incidental or consequential damages arising directly or indirectly from the use of any of the information contained in this book.

The Heart of Stable Relationships: 12 ways the Healing Power of Horses Can Transform Your Life.

Reviews

"Knowledge is power. Awareness is liberating and the Truth sets us free." These three phrases in Chapter 12 sum it up. A heart warming, authentic, thought provoking book that transforms the relationships in your life in a way you never imagined possible . . . especially the relationship with yourself! As a Horsemanship Coach, I witness the effect horses and humans have on each other every day. The combination of working with the horses and embracing the Spiritual Truths that Wendy shares in this book are very powerful . . . very powerful indeed!

Monica Andréewitch Horsemanship Coach

Written with great depth and insight Wendy and the horses take you on a journey through yourself. Her personal experiences, case studies and exercises give rise to an inner understanding which can be used to transcend everything which holds you back in life, releasing past limitations and literally reach and live the world of your dreams. Xxx

Ruth Coldspring Professional Hairdresser

The HEART of Stable Relationships is a wonderful insight into the true relationships and interactions between horses and humans. This truly amazing book highlights the beauty these highly intuitive horses can bring to your personal life, aiding to self discovery and unfolding the real truths long buried, deeply denied or merely unaware of. Unearthing your deepest insecurities and traits—one naturally prefers to suppress—it allows you to explore and understand your true self.

All this achieved in glorious surroundings with the generosity of non-judgemental horses whom themselves possess their own special, unique personalities and characteristics. Wendy captures and displays how new found wisdom and freedoms can be revealed. Ditched are the weighted shackles, instead they are replaced with purer energy and clarity, sharing with you how day-to-day relationships can be met with a healthier approach.

Wendy has captured the magic and embodiment to truly change your life by getting up close and personal with horses and the beauty being . . . it maybe your first ever experience with these majestic animals, you certainly won't want it to be your last.

Hayley Corcoran Surrey

Wendy has created a book that is as profound and life changing as the fascinating work I have witnessed again and again with her beloved herd and the humans they transform. Wendy weaves her magic inspiring us page by page to honour ourselves and those who share this precious journey of life. It will warm your heart, touch your Soul and transform your relationships. Simply wonderful!

Elaine Wilkins founder The Chrysalis Effect ME,
CFS and Fibromyalgia Recovery.

The HEART of Stable Relationships is a great tool IF you're ready to change and heal, but what makes it exceptional is that it is a <u>collaboration forged in the unconditional love</u> that only animals can give. I love this book because in it, Wendy shares how horses teach us how to be better, more balanced, loving beings, just as she does in person in her program. Although changing is never easy, in these pages you can ride with caring horses, unconditionally supported on the road to wholeness. Go for it!

Kate Solisti Internationally renown
Interspecies Communicator

Watch your own relationships flourish as Wendy's profound yet practical teachings guide you to establish stability, trust and teamwork in your life.

Kelly McKain Best Selling Author

Table of Contents

Acknowledgements v
Foreword vii
Note To The Reader ix
Case Studies at a glance xvii
About the Author xix

Introduction 1

Chapter 1: **If wishes were horses . . .**
　　　　　　You had better believe it 7

Chapter 2: **Mirror, mirror on the wall . . .**
　　　　　　are you a bit of a dark horse after all? 22

Chapter 3: **Hold your horses!**
　　　　　　Are you controlling your emotions?
　　　　　　Or are your emotions controlling you? 34

Chapter 4: **Getting Back in the Saddle**
　　　　　　Overcoming fears, fantasies and phobias 46

Chapter 5:	**Straight from the horse's mouth**	
	Non-Verbal Communication is the loudest........ 60	
Chapter 6:	**Wild Horses couldn't drag me away . . .**	
	Healing the heart of childhood challenges 67	
Chapter 7:	**Get down off your high horse!**	
	Do you want to be right or happy?....................... 74	
Chapter 8:	**You can lead a horse to water but you can't make them drink**	
	(Or you can lead a partner to relationship, But you can't make them commit) 90	
Chapter 9:	**It's no good flogging a dead horse**	
	Is it time to commit or quit? 99	
Chapter 10:	**Unbridled Passion**	
	Do what you love, love what you do 106	
Chapter 11:	**Loving Leadership**	
	Finding your authentic place in the herd of life 117	
Chapter 12:	**Stride to Success**	
	The Spiritual Purpose of Relationships 125	

Case Studies at a glance

Case Study 1: Unlucky in love 12
Case Study 2: The Alchemy of Archer 14
Case Study 3: Smartie and Self Belief 16
Case Study 4: Whose aggression is whose? 26
Case Study 5: Bosses behaving badly 28
Case Study 6: Angst in the Air 36
Case Study 7: Emotional Control 37
Case Study 8: Strong Silent Support 39
Case Study 9: Magic touch 42
Case Study 10: Trapped and Trampled 48
Case Study 11: You can have it all 54
Case Study 12: Boosting Boundaries 56
Case Study 13: Say what you mean, mean what you say 62
Case Study 14: Attack causes defence 64
Case Study 15: The Invisible Lady 68
Case Study 16: Abandoning the belief 70
Case Study 17: Typical Tactics 72

Case Study 18: Toxic Tone 75
Case Study 19: When you are in control you don't
                          need to be 78
Case Study 20: Trying to control the uncontrollable 80
Case Study 21: Is breaking up hard to do? 94
Case Study 22: It's a dog's life 96
Case Study 23: Distant relationship 100
Case Study 24: The importance of being Earnest 101
Case Study 25: Unavailable, Unsuitable, Unwilling 104
Case Study 26: Depression to Elation 108
Case Study 27: It is not your partner stopping you 109
Case Study 28: Rosie, Riding and Wrists 113
Case Study 29: The truth will out itself 114
Case Study 30: A little less conversation,
                          a little more action 119
Case Study 31: Going round and round in circles 120
Case Study 32: Out of Balance 128
Case Study 33: The good the bad and the not so ugly 130

About the Author

Wendy Felicity Firmin-Price H.E.A.R.T. (Holistic Equine Assisted Relationship Transformation) Equine Assisted Therapy Practitioner. B.H.S.I.(T) Metaphysical Supervisor, Teacher and Spiritual Life Mentor.

With over 30 years of experience, Wendy is a pioneer in the practice and teaching of the holistic approach to horse riding and equine assisted therapy, and in 1990's became one of the first teachers promoting this powerful tool in the UK. Her personal journey in reaching this point in her career is both the reason and the means by which she discovered the approach. Her own experiences of the change it brought about in her life and riding created a life-long commitment to sharing these methods with others.

Wendy was bought her first pony when she was 12 years old and had him for 30 years when he sadly passed on. After leaving school Wendy worked in a variety of environments, then in 1984 she began work in a horse 'livery' yard. The demand for her to teach riding created the need for her to set up a 'traditional' riding school. The school was a great success and in 1990 Wendy passed her professional riding and BHS Intermediate Teaching exams.

Wendy's personal life however was far from perfect. She

found herself drawn into dysfunctional relationships, her self-esteem was low, she suffered a lack of confidence and feared many things - including the jumping she would need to do in order to pass her riding exam. In her quest to resolve the personal issues that were holding her back, Wendy learned about Metaphysics. She made the link between using a metaphysical approach for dealing with one life situation to dealing with the fear of clearing a show-jump. The results were a great success. This led her on to further valuable research in which she used the same techniques with her existing riding clients - again, with remarkable results.

The outcome of this gave her an even greater understanding of the partnerships between horse and rider and the parallels that gives them in their personal relationships and lives.

Wendy's commitment to the process led her to complete a Metaphysical Practitioner and Teacher course and she is currently the only riding instructor in the UK to have a Teaching Diploma in Practical Metaphysics. Her approach to 'Holistic Riding' has also been covered in many magazines, national press and radio stations including Radio 4's 'All in the Mind'. Through developing her unique approach Wendy has put into practise her philosophies to move through many life challenges. Just some of these include overcoming M.E. many addictions, stress, self-sabotage, low self-esteem, blocked emotions, eating disorders, financial debts, loss of confidence and relationship problems.

Whilst going through these experiences she has noticed the various effects they have had on her riding, horses and relationships. Discovering that horses revealed to her more about how to have relationship success than any other therapy Wendy has now put together the HEART programme (which stands for Holistic Equine Assisted Relationship Transformation) and is a series of workshops and courses. Through working therapeutically with the horses all types of relationships can be improved and transformed. Wendy offers privates sessions, workshops and trains other people to become HEART Equine Facilitators and Coaches.

Wendy's unusual blend of qualifications, personal experiences, compassion and humour allow her to mentor, guide and inspire others to be more confident, enjoy their relationships with horses and people and live the lives they truly want.

There is no problem greater than the Power within you to overcome it!

Wendyism

Introduction

My childhood sweetheart

I was walking down the country lane in Ockham with my not so tall but very dark, and certainly handsome, love of my life. I had been in love with him for 30 years. We were more than just childhood sweethearts. We had been together since my 12th birthday, when I just knew that we were going to be together for life.

Over the years he had seen me at my best – and at my worst. He got me through my troubled and painful childhood. I had cried so many times on his shoulder. He used to just stand there, quietly understanding and miraculously soothing my sadness. You would definitely describe him as the strong silent type.

I never detected any jealousy from him regarding my other boyfriends. However, when I was with them I was in a very different type of relationship. With all my relationships, I felt as though I was forever trying to get the other person to love me. I guess none of them measured up to the real love of my life and I always went back to him. I never felt I had to earn my worthiness or love from him, it flowed naturally and unconditionally.

I could totally be myself with him. It seemed he knew my every thought. I never felt judged, just accepted. It was reciprocated as there was nothing I wouldn't do for him and to keep us together. It had been, and always will be, my most stable relationship.

His name? Tiggy. Well actually, when I first had him he was called Trigger. A little black Welsh Mountain pony. "Hang on," I hear you say "I thought I'd bought a book on relationships. What has a pony got to do with relationships?" Everything, I eventually discovered.

Everything I learnt about the art of relationships and communication

Tiggy and my herd of horses taught me.

On this particular day, when I was walking with him, I had asked: "How is it that we have been together for 30 years and it has hardly seemed like a day and that commitment has been so easy and effortless with you? Yet, when I even think of committing to a man, I am filled with dread, start to sweat and want to run a mile?" I swear this is what I *heard* him reply:

"Oh, that's easy to answer. Throughout my life you've given unconditionally to me. Your love, your desire for me to have the best in life, has made you selfless. You have always accepted me just as I am and for what I can or can't give you. You've never tried to change me; you have just accepted me completely as I am."

To this day I don't know if I actually did *hear* him talk to me or whether it was my own thoughts answering, or maybe it was a deep insight that had popped in to my mind. Either way, it was the biggest turning point in my life and my relationships. Looking back on that moment, as I was literally standing at the crossroads in that country lane, I realise now it was symbolic of the crossroads I had reached in my life and relationships.

Up until that point I had been through many relationships, not quite as many as the hot dinners I'd had but certainly a lot.

I had never got past the two year mark and I remember I had vowed in childhood that I would never marry. My experience of marriage and relationships was rather tainted. *Every relationship around me had ended, or was ending in disaster or divorce.* Most of my own relationships had been abusive or dysfunctional in some way.

When my own mum and dad acrimoniously split up I was extremely bewildered, thinking, as most children do, that I had done something wrong or that I was no longer loveable. Then when my mum ended up with an abusive partner I lost even more faith in marriage or meaningful relationships.

The only good thing that came out of my parents' divorce was that my new stepfather tried to buy his way into my affections by purchasing my little black pony, Trigger. I have no idea how my life would have turned out without my little black, woolly, four footed therapist and relationship guru. I am, though, completely convinced that he saved me from sliding into quite a dark world in my childhood.

Crossroads of my life

So, back to the crossroads where I was standing with Tiggy. I pondered my revelation and thought about my relationship with my partner at the time. John was a very patient, loving man who I had been with for quite a while, after a very traumatic and melodramatic dysfunctional relationship. Did I love him unconditionally? If I am honest, not really at the time. My attitude was: if I did this for him, I expected him to do that for me. Did I accept him as he was? No, of course not. I was here to change him into a better man - after all wasn't that my job? Did I want the best for him? Yes, but I wanted my needs to be met first. I had a lot to learn!

I want to share with you the wisdom and insights that I have gained along the way. They took me from an abusive violent relationship to the most wonderful man, who I have been with for over 20 years. What is different about this wisdom is that it has been reinforced and explained in a way that intellectual knowledge can't match.

Horses bring theory alive

It is one thing to read that changing your thoughts will change your life. It is another to get instant proof that when you change your mind-set you get instant feedback *and results.*

Even if you're not into horses, there is wonderful wisdom to be gained from the following pages, which can help bring more peace, harmony and love into your life and relationships.

So how does this book differ from other relationship manuals? There are hundreds of publications about relationships but this book gives a completely different insight. It is based on studying horses in a domestic setting and observing how the herd creates harmony and how humans can benefit from their 'secrets' to improve relationships. If you combine these revelations with the little known powers of the Universe you can transform anything - your relationships, life, career and confidence. I have personally researched all of these!

This isn't going to be a book about how to play psychological games to catch your man or about how to manipulate people in a relationship. Instead, the horses invite you to find your authentic self. Something that can get lost in all the roles, duties and plate-spinning some of you feel you have to do.

If you are a woman it's not about burning your bra, becoming completely independent or overly dependent. Or, if you are a man, it's not about having to hug a tree to get in touch with your feminine feelings.

This is about how you can restore, rejuvenate or start afresh the relationships in your lives. It is about empowering you to be ok with yourself and to not need those relationships or roles to validate who you are. To get to the point of feeling wonderful *with* or *without* people illustrates true power, confidence and self-love.

Introduction

This is about changing your life:

From mediocre to magical, haphazard to harmonious, lonely to full of love.

My own study of horses' social structure and how their herd dynamics create a successful way to interact with one another, has uncovered lots of secrets and clues that can be translated to human relationships.

For example, it is interesting that in the wild there are very few fights between horses, even between stallions. Fights tend to break out only when there is a resource challenge. If we look at fights among humans isn't that exactly what is happening for us? There is a belief there is not enough money, love, opportunity, etc. The aim of a balanced herd of horses is to live peacefully and harmoniously with one another. What a great goal to aspire to!

Horses have evolved and stayed alive for over 64,000,000 million years. Pretty good going for a prey animal at the top of the food chain! Their success in not being woofed down by a pack of wolves or becoming a tasty tenderloin steak for a tiger is what we want to explore. They have even managed to adapt to a lifestyle we humans have imposed on them and still survived.

As interaction between horses and humans has increased we have been able to learn from their wisdom, optimism and patience. Few people can watch a herd of running horses without being stirred by their majestic energy, beauty and strength.

The stories throughout this book are real, although in some cases, for reasons of confidentiality names or professions may have been changed to avoid identification. It will be a little difficult to really portray the magic and transformation that happens. The best way is to book a session or attend a workshop and experience first-hand the healing and inspiration our horses can share with you.

It's worth noting that, while all horses respond to energy around them, not all horses are suited to a regular therapeutic or coaching environment. We feel it is imperative that the horse gives us permission to work with a particular human. At the end of each session we give gratitude to the horses. They also have a regular holistic therapy support programme to ensure they haven't taken on board any of our human baggage.

Thankfully, having a large herd, we always have a willing selection of horses to choose from and sometimes the horses themselves make it very clear who they want to work with or not!

Read on to learn how to take back the reins of control of your life.

Ways to use the book:

1. Enjoy reading the book from cover to cover.
2. Think of a challenge you have with a specific relationship. Then choose a number between 1-12. That chapter may give you some insights.
3. Choose a number between 1-33 and find the case study with that number. Perhaps that person's experience might help you.
4. Ask for inspiration from your Inner Wisdom and just open the book at the page you get drawn to and explore the information written.
5. Take advantage of the many bonus offers throughout the book and come and experience for yourself how the Healing Power of Horses could transform your life.

CHAPTER 1

If wishes were horses . . . You had better believe it

IMAGINE A SOCIETY THAT VALUES harmony above all else. Picture a community where everyone looks out for each other and has concern for group safety, not just their own. Think about how easy life would be if everyone used the same clear, consistent code of communication.

From my experience, horses in a stable herd exhibit behaviour that epitomises stability, trust and teamwork. They reveal the art of honest communication and, above all, they can show us humans how to live peacefully and harmoniously. At the HEART Centre (Holistic Equine Assisted Relationship Transformation), we provide the opportunity for you to observe and learn from an animal which, let's face it, is happy to spend most of its time standing around in a field eating grass, regardless of the weather!

Balance of Power

Horses primarily express the feminine energy of empathy, instinct and gentleness, yet also have the ability to use their masculine energy to be aggressive, powerful and decisive. Their communication with themselves and each other is clear, which combined with their connection to nature, allows them to trust one another with their lives. They are connected to their authentic power in a balanced way. By working with these majestic creatures you too can learn the secrets of how to balance your own masculine and feminine power which is the key to the HEART of successful relationships and communication.

Take a moment to explore the relationships you have in your life. Can you trust your partner with your life? Can your partner trust you with theirs? Are you able to say that of your boss, or of yourself? What about relationships with your work colleagues, family, friends? Who would you turn to for support? Would you be the one everyone looks to for guidance?

Think about the relationship with yourself: can you depend on yourself? Or, do you abandon yourself in a crisis?

You are always in relationship...

. . . with something, someone or yourself. You have relationships with people (family, friends & foes), places, money, time, food, health, your environment, your car, your home – everything. Each of these relationships is influenced by your beliefs. In fact your experiences around any form of relationships come about from the concepts you hold.

Whatever you believe about relationships – you are right!
Wendyism

What are beliefs?

Beliefs are a collection of thoughts, which you make an assumption about. These thoughts usually come from experiences you've had or observations you've made throughout your life.

Your thoughts become your thinking. Your thinking creates your beliefs. Your beliefs develop into concepts.

Thoughts → Thinking → Beliefs → Concepts

Thoughts are tangible

Consider this concept as being the root of all your experiences of relationships. Your thoughts are powerful. Whatever beliefs you have regarding relationships will be the result of your experience. This applies to all types of relationship – money, work, health, happiness, romance, success, life, self, family. You name it, somewhere along the line you have developed a belief about the relationship you have with it.

Initially thoughts are neutral. They float around the atmosphere like pollen or radio waves. When you engage with thoughts they start to become a part of you and that produces a line of thinking. Sometimes these lines of thinking don't go anywhere, a bit like being in a maze, or they may take you off in a particular direction.

When these thoughts and thinking are the result of certain events that you've experienced or witnessed, you start to string these thoughts along to make beliefs. Before you know it, you've created concepts, opinions and assumptions.

What are you thinking?

The average person has approximately 66,000 thoughts per day. These thoughts are like thousands of seeds blowing in the wind, landing in different types of soils. Some never take root; some get overtaken by other plants; some seeds are left unattended while others are given lots of attention and grow.

These 'thought seeds' always have an opportunity to grow into something. So, wherever you put and tend your thoughts, these 'seeds' will come to fruition. Your mind is like the soil: just as the soil doesn't determine what is a weed or a flower but responds the same to both, so too does your mind. Just for poetic licence let us call the more limiting, negative, fearful thoughts 'weeds' and your expanding, positive and loving thoughts 'beautiful plants'.

Event, Emotion, Experience

Here is an example of an assumption that a typical 10 year old girl might make about relationships when her mum and dad split up.

Event: Parents split up but don't explain to her what is happening.

Thought: Dad hasn't contacted me for ages (neutral at this point).

Thinking: I wonder what happened. Mum seems sad. Did I do something wrong?

Belief: My dad doesn't love me. I am unwanted. It must have been my fault. I can't control anything.

Emotion Beliefs now set up a chain of emotions and feelings like guilt, hurt, sadness, bewilderment, anger and confusion.

Assumption: I must have done something wrong. I am unlovable. I am to blame.

Concepts: Men reject me. Relationships don't last. I am guilty.

Life events attracted: Relationships not lasting; people frequently rejecting her; low self-esteem from feeling unlovable, probably resulting in abusive or dysfunctional relationships in one form or another. Unable to set appropriate boundaries for fear of rejection.

Just that one childhood event could massively influence her whole life. Imagine all the erroneous beliefs you may have taken on board since your childhood.

Exercise 1: What are your thoughts, beliefs and assumptions about relationships?

Do you believe you will get hurt, betrayed or rejected?

Do you believe it's not safe to trust?

Do you believe that it's best not to commit in case something better comes along?

Do you *really* love your partner or do you **need** your partner?

Do you believe your partner is there to meet your needs or be in sacrifice to theirs?

Do you believe there should be a happily ever after? Or that love is just for fairy tales?

Do you believe you can't have the relationship and career you want?

Do you believe you can't be your true self in a relationship?

What is the connection between horses and my relationships?

If you aren't sure of your beliefs around relationships when you work with horses you'll find out almost instantly. Every thought, belief and thinking process carries its own magnetic energy field. Einstein proved that everything boils down to energy. So, when you have particular thoughts you attract an experience to back up the energy produced by these thoughts. However, when it comes to encounters with humans, although the same thing happens and we attract certain events, people and challenges into our lives, some of us are completely unaware of what we're attracting.

When you work with animals, especially with horses, you learn that they provide instant feedback on your energy field by how they react to you. It's a fascinating process: the horse you get drawn to, or not, is able to reveal your overriding beliefs. Horses can highlight the needs, expectations and desires you have from relationships.

As human beings, we do the same but we misunderstand the feedback we get from our relationships and often label other people as the problem. Or, we wonder why we keep getting rejected or have a need to control.

One of the most common patterns of behaviour we see, especially among women, is that they will do anything to try and get the horse to like them. Rather than set appropriate boundaries if the horse has its own agenda, they often appease, beg or give up. They just do not believe strongly enough that their needs matter too. When the horse backs off from these people's energy or vibration, this can bring up all sorts of hidden patterns and pain within them.

Case Study 1: Unlucky in love

An exercise in one workshop was to choose a horse to work with. One lady went round all the horses but each one she chose was unavailable in some way. It was either lame, belonged to someone else or was about to go into a lesson. She selected about five unavailable horses. When she did get to choose a horse that was available she had difficulty in getting him to do the exercises. She found bonding with the horse a challenge.

When gently asked how this might be a pattern in her relationships, she couldn't immediately see the connection. Her friend, who had come with her, let out an almighty gasp when he suddenly got the connection. He named all the unavailable men she'd been involved with, at which point she understood the horse's behaviour. She hadn't noticed her pattern over the years and had convinced herself that she had just had a run of bad luck in relationships and was unlucky in love. She held very limiting beliefs about relationships.

Beliefs self-perpetuate: you make a belief from one experience and that belief has to attract an experience to back it up. You end up with a string of experiences that reinforce the belief.

Your beliefs co-create your reality

As described earlier, your thoughts and beliefs sow the seeds of your experience of reality. If you believe you will get hurt in a relationship you can't produce anything else but proof that you're right by setting up an experience that hurts you. Your mind always proves you right because it has no power to do otherwise. It's just as powerless as planting the soil with an onion bulb and expecting a daffodil to grow.

Change your beliefs to change your reality

To change your experience you must change your thinking to what you want to have as your reality. This is not about manipulating people but changing the scripts you assign to them. Neither is this about trying to change or control people: when you have an expanded view of someone and see them with a loving open heart your experiences become very different.

Case Study 2: The Alchemy of Archer

Archer was a stunning 14.3 hands high (h.h.) piebald gelding. When he arrived he came with *Attitude* with a capital A. It was through no fault of his own because he hadn't been used to freedom or being with other horses (he'd been taken away too early from his mum and sibling herd) so he had never really learnt 'horse talk' (Equus). When he joined my stable herd, all hell let loose and within a week Archer had gained a reputation among us humans for being the devil horse and I'm sure probably some similar sentiments from the horses.

He was not only aggressive and bolshie towards all the other horses but was just as pushy and in your face with humans. Unfortunately, the more people projected their fears, beliefs and concepts about Archer onto him, the more those thoughts, beliefs and behaviour were acted out by him. (Think angry teenager with no stability at home or boundaries). The worse he got, the more frightened people became of dealing with him.

I quickly called a staff meeting and explained that we needed to change our beliefs about Archer urgently. We had to project onto Archer how we *wanted* him to behave and to give praise and attention *as soon as he exhibited even the tiniest effort towards our projections*. When he behaved in a way that was unhelpful to him, other horses or people we completely ignored both Archer and the behaviour.

Interestingly, this is exactly what the rest of the herd did. They kept removing themselves from him and the mares would send him out of the herd and leave him on his own. For a prey animal this is a very vulnerable position to be in. Safety in numbers is their motto!

However, within less than a week he started to change and over the next month the lovely Archer completely altered his behaviour and attitude towards the other horses and humans. He became amenable, willing to please and great to be around. He soon found a pair bond (firm friend) in the herd and settled down.

He still had his spirit and Archer was Archer: we certainly wouldn't have wanted him any other way. He kept us on our toes to make sure that what we were thinking or projecting onto him was the message we actually wanted him to get. He became more peaceful and allowed his sense of humour to flow through.

In truth we hadn't changed the humans or horses per se; we had changed our concept of, in this instance, the horse. Because that concept and assumption *is* now different they *have to act* differently. "But he's like that with everyone," I hear you say. Yes, because everyone has bought into the same belief about that person or horse. Unless someone is consciously aware they are caught up in someone else's script or concept there is very little power they can have against it.

Thoughts are powerful

There were two groups of teachers and each was given a class of children. One group was told that their class was really brainy and the other group was told that their kids were useless and just marking time until they were able to leave school.

So which kids excelled? The ones that the teachers thought were really brainy. However, what is really interesting is that the classes had been swapped around and it was the so-called slower children that excelled. The brainy children didn't do very well because nobody believed they could.

At the HEART Centre, when children with challenging behaviour, or who have been excluded from school, come to work therapeutically with the horses, the key thing I impress on my facilitators and the support workers is that we don't want to be told about the kid's background or story. My facilitators have to be just like the horses and take the children at face value, with no preconceived ideas. I want them to see the kids in pure innocence.

When horses come into contact with a person, child or another horse, they don't meet with a label and that is why their connection is truer. Horses just take that person as they are on that particular day. What horses do is to note the energy field and emotions that person is carrying around them and respond accordingly.

Case Study 3: Smartie and Self Belief

On several occasions, we have had the wonderful opportunity to work with organisations that support vulnerable adults and troubled teenagers. One time a perplexed lad was drawn to Smartie. Smartie had started his life with quite a verbally abusive owner who never had a good word to say about this innocent little pony. She was always saying how useless he was, would never give him any praise even when he managed to do something right. She had no belief in him whatsoever. In human terms he came to me with very little esteem and loss of confidence in himself. This would make him very anxious when he was being ridden and the moment he got worried or confused his behaviour would appear very disruptive, aggressive or unmanageable.

Just as I have described Smartie's background, we later discovered that this was the identical story of the young lad who had been drawn to him.

Over the course of our 12 week programme that we offered, the transformation of this boisterous boy was absolutely amazing. While he was at the stables, he learnt for the first time how to become calm. When he worked with Smartie he learnt the value of boundaries and why they had to be in place for their own safety. He discovered what it felt like when Smartie was being disruptive and unco-operative. He came to the realisation that this must be what his fellow friends, teachers and support workers felt too, when he himself was behaving in a similar way. His support workers were truly astounded.

Most importantly, each week as he succeeded with the tasks alongside Smartie, his own self-belief improved which in turn increased his self-confidence. To back up the positive experiences these children were having, we invited the support workers to start really changing their beliefs, not just about this young lad but all their charges. They began to see just how important that was to be consistent.

You can only receive to the level you believe

When you start to change your thinking and beliefs the most important aspect initially is to have a degree of believability in your beliefs. Otherwise, when you affirm your new beliefs to yourself you will have another voice arguing that it's not true. This is equivalent to sowing a weed with every new seed. The wording has to be carefully chosen and resistances to the new belief flushed out.

Exercise 2: What your mind can conceive and believe you can readily achieve

Take a moment to think about a relationship you would like to transform, change or improve. If you're not sure about which relationship to transform, here's a free downloadable exercise to help you get clarity: www.theheartofstablerelationships.com/Bonusexercise1

What beliefs, assumptions or concepts do you currently have around this relationship?

What beliefs might you be projecting onto this relationship?

In other words, have you *actually* been rejected, betrayed or hurt or is that simply your belief?

What are your biggest fears about this relationship?

Now change these beliefs into the positive, present and personal. (For a full description of this exercise visit www.theheartofstablerelationships.com/bonusexercise2 for another of your free bonuses on how to change limiting beliefs.)

If you could record these thoughts, what would they mainly be focused on: the past or the future?

If you watch our herd of horses you will see that, for the most part, their stability comes from just observing and noticing what is going on around them. They read the energies of the weather, people and environment and respond accordingly – *in the moment*. That is not to say that their past issues do not affect them but just not quite in the same way as humans. Horses do not fret about the future in the way that humans do.

However, if we took away their freedom to eat, to move, be pain free, safe and carry out their normal daily functions the horses' reactions would immediately change. Then you would see irritable, stressed and anxious horses. It's interesting to note that horses would mirror the same instability and insecurity you might experience if your resources were limited.

Visualise, verbalise, vitalise

The key to getting new beliefs to work for you is to start wearing them and acting as if they were true. Beliefs carry energetic vibrations which is why working with horses is powerful as they are able to recognise these vibrations.

To horses, everything has an energy. If we remember the devastating tsunami event a few years ago, there were amazing stories about animals appearing to go wild and making for the hills beforehand. There were a couple of stories that really stood out for me. A tame elephant near a hotel complex suddenly picked up a young child, who'd been playing around the elephants, with its trunk and ran off. At first, people thought the elephant had gone berserk and many ran after it trying to stop the elephant. Those people survived.

Another account involved a party of people who were diving. The instructor noticed all the sea animals were going in the same direction and, thinking quickly, persuaded the deep sea party to follow. Again those people survived.

Even with my own herd of horses I can tell when a bit of a storm is brewing as they go from peacefully grazing to dashing to the wind-breaking hedges way before the storm actually arrives.

Personal anecdote:
You have the power to change anything

Along my life's path of researching relationships, one of my chapters was with a perplexed soul who in his *dis*ease of drinking became very violent. Unfortunately, due to my own lack of self-worth, boundaries and self-love, I allowed myself to be his punch bag.

During this time, I was led to *You Can Heal Your Life* by Louise Hay, a self-help book. I learnt to affirm: "I now deserve to have a wonderful loving partner who treats me well." If I had affirmed that "K now stops beating me and loves me," I would have been trying to exercise control over another person.

As my self-esteem slowly increased I found the courage to finally say: "I love and accept you for who you are. However, if you have a need to continue to be violent towards me we have to end our relationship." I could love him but not his behaviour.

All my previous attempts at trying to finish with him had never been said with conviction or had never been followed through by me. This time I had a new sense of self-worth and when, sadly, he chose to take his inner pain out on me again, I finally found the courage to walk away. I was unable to control K and now, instead of allowing him to control me, I got out of my victim mode and took control of myself and my life.

Incidentally, the outcome of my new belief was that I do now have a wonderful, loving husband who treats me exceptionally well. We have been together happily for over 20 years!

Fake it 'til you make it

Act as if your beliefs were already true.....

What would that look like? In what way would you be altered? How would your day be different? How would you feel? (More about feelings in chapter 3). Even if you cannot fully implement the changes needed, start to make small changes in your day and yourself which will signal to your consciousness that you have a new belief in place that needs proving right.

Visualise your life as you would like it to be

Verbalise your new beliefs by saying them out loud. Sing them

Vitalise them. Give energy and excitement to them. Dance them

Let go of the need for life to happen in a certain way

The greatest pain in life comes from arguing with reality, resisting change and fighting to control the uncontrollable. When you *demand* or believe the relationship you want to transform or manifest *has* to be a certain way, you limit the way that life can do its magic. I wholeheartedly believe that we live in a truly amazing Universe. Not only is every snowflake unique but so is every blade of grass. The planets are not just in mathematical order; apparently they are in musical arrangement too. You cannot possibly know how events will unfold. One of the first steps to creating stability in your life and relationships with time, money or people is to let go of your plans. After all, have they worked so far?

Healing Power of Horses Principle 1

"The surest way to maketh man
Is to positively think him so.
Do the same for you or your horse
And a fine friend you'll have, not foe"
Wendyism

CHAPTER 2

Mirror, mirror on the wall . . . are you a bit of a dark horse after all?

HAVE YOU EVER WONDERED WHY certain people push your buttons? Or, why you keep attracting the same type of partner or boss? Have you noticed that even when you have moved miles away the same sort of challenges crop up when dealing with people? Most of us are familiar with pets looking like their owners but have you ever noticed how they are often like them in character as well, or their absolute opposite?

Well, none of this is by chance. There is a Universal Law that states that the world is a mirror of your mind. This is called the Law of Reflection. This law tends to work alongside the Law of Attraction.

The Law of Reflection was one of the first laws I learnt when I was discovering metaphysics and a more spiritual way of life. At the time I was experiencing major drama in my life and relationships. My horses were constantly getting into fights and three of them ended up with very serious injuries and kicks.

One of them was my darling little pony, Pepsi. A stunning little chestnut pony that was extremely popular with the kids. Unfortunately, he got badly kicked which resulted in a chipped shoulder bone.

My personal relationship at the time was also very violent and full of melodrama. My financial life was equally volatile and I was sinking rapidly into serious debt (although my day-to-day life was so chaotic that I was completely unaware of how bad my financial situation had become).

I had a couple of horses that were completely out of control and impossible to ride. Trezzy, in particular, had no brakes whatsoever. Even getting the two of us out of the yard was always a major drama: there were tears and tantrums when I tried to stay on as she reared and spun round. Talk about having my perfect mirror!

Can you imagine then how I felt when I came across *You Can Heal Your Life* by Louise Hay and read the opening lines about how we all create our own reality and that people are our mirrors? Well, I didn't just think her suggestions were ridiculous, I threw the book away! If we *really* could create our own reality who on earth in their right mind would choose to create such a chaotic, melodramatic debt-ridden life and to live with a violent drunk?

Although I chucked the book out, annoyingly I couldn't get rid of my thoughts. Her words kept echoing through my mind. What did she mean by stating you can create your own reality? You can really heal your own life? What if I really could change my life by altering my thinking? Having played the victim most of my life that was going to be a tall order for such a short woman but the prospect was attractive. The idea that I really could change my life made me more and more curious.

However, I drew the line at people being my reflection. After all I didn't drink, I didn't lie, I wasn't dishonest, I wasn't angry and I certainly wasn't violent. I was Miss Goody Two Shoes. Well, at least that was the persona I liked to portray.

As I learnt more about the Laws of Attraction and Reflection,

I was absolutely horrified to realise that while those personality traits may have been what I portrayed outwardly, the way I treated myself was marked by constant self-attack. (You know that incessant voice in your head that goes on and on, saying: "you're not good enough….what makes you think you are lovable. What right do you have be successful and happy?" etc.)

I was constantly beating myself up for not being good enough. I may not have been an alcoholic but I was certainly addicted to lots of other things, such as work, chaos and debt. I may not have been dishonest in business but I was dishonest with myself and even with others about how I was really feeling and what was going on in my life.

As for fooling myself that I wasn't an angry person, I discovered that I was so disassociated from my anger that I needed an abusive relationship to show me just how much I was raging inside. That little pony Pepsi, with the chip in his shoulder, was symbolic of the huge boulder that was on my shoulder that I'd unwittingly been carrying since childhood. What was happening with the horses was a direct reflection of the outward violence from my partner and the self-attack within me.

> **"Truth goes through three stages,**
> **Firstly, it is ridiculed,**
> **Secondly, it is violently opposed**
> **Thirdly, it is accepted as being self-evident."**
> **Arthur Schopenhauer**

I certainly had ridiculed the book at first and then I violently opposed it by chucking it out but oh what a difference it made to my life when I allowed its words to become self-evident. My horses were definitely testament to my state of consciousness. The other Spiritual Statement of "The Truth shall set you free" certainly unlocked my door to freedom.

Wherever you go, there you are

The Law of Reflection also supports the spiritual philosophy that you, me and everyone else are all one. We're like an ocean with many waves or, my favourite analogy, a giant mirror disco ball. Individually, we are all the different facets that make up that ball.

People, life, horses and situations will reflect back to you:

- the things you love about yourself or life
- the things you dislike and despise about yourself or life
- the things you believe about yourself or life
- the areas where you are out of balance
- your patterns of survival
- emotions that need healing
- the scripts that you have assigned people
- The parts of you that you have disassociated from.

Me and my shadow

This is the part of yourself that you really don't want to admit to having. You would die with embarrassment/shame if someone knew you were like that. It's the part of yourself that you suppress or disassociate from in the hope that you won't have to encounter it or admit that it is a part of you.

Unconsciously this part of you then gets projected outside of you onto another person or, if you're working with the HEART Centre, a horse. Either will act out the characteristic you dislike about yourself or are disassociated from. Looking at what was happening with the horses I could see that their unruly behaviour was a reflection of the turmoil in my own life.

Case Study 4: Whose aggression is whose?

I went to see a client about a horse that couldn't be handled when doing certain essential tasks. This very quiet, patient and kind gentleman was having trouble with the staff where he had his horse.

The horse was acting really aggressively and quite violently every day. He would turn round and lash out and if that didn't work he would spin his head sideways and, with his teeth, take a chunk out of you. This was one angry horse.

We explored some practical tips, talked to the staff about changing their beliefs about the horse but then, as I dug a bit deeper, the owner confessed he didn't mind his horse acting this way. I was really curious. His reason was that although he was a very placid person, there was a deeper part of him that really wished he could let his anger out like his horse did.

I explained that in order to really help his horse he had to get in touch with his own anger and heal and integrate it into his own personality so that his horse wouldn't have to do his anger work for him.

The horse was expressing what we call his shadow self. The gentleman could not express his own anger and had become disassociated from it. In this case the horse acted out the part of him he so desperately wanted to, but was too afraid to, express.

For the moment, let us continue to understand the Law of Reflection and how it works.

It's easy to see the nice bits in others like kindness, being loving and helpful. You probably won't have much difficulty in seeing the nice bits of yourself in others too. But, what about when we see someone acting in a disagreeable way, how can that be a reflection of ourselves?

A common example I use is the 'selfish side'. Let's face it, you don't want to be called or be known as selfish. So what tends to happen is you suppress this part and rather than admit you have a selfish side you do the complete opposite and go into sacrifice. The degree to which we go into disassociation from one side of the pendulum is the degree to which we go into compensation on the other.

Nature always seeks balance. In order to balance your self-sacrificing part, you will attract to you someone who can act out the part of being selfish. The degree to which you are in sacrifice is the degree to which they will be in selfishness.

"You can't change the reflection by changing the mirror."
Wendyism

As you can't change the other person or insist they act differently, you have to be the one who makes the first change. *You* have to make the change inwardly for it to be outwardly different. You have to integrate or accept the aspect of you that the other person is reflecting. When you do, the sorts of changes that you are likely to experience are that the person:

- leaves or moves out of your circle (they no longer need to be your balancing rod or mirror or shadow self)
- moves into balance to the degree you do (think of a see-saw or pair of sprung scales)

Or:
- the person's behaviour no longer has any effect on you
- you cease to have any emotional reactions to the situation (if you do there is still integration work to be done).

So, how can you use the Law of Reflection to your advantage? I will share with you how I use it. First, I always look to see how my horses are behaving or reacting. They are my life barometer. When I am reasonably in balance they reflect that by being healthy, happy and behaving well. When there is something going on within me, which I'm typically unaware of, they usually act that out.

Boris is a prime reflector of when I am feeling resistant to life. When I resist moving forward not getting on with writing my book or attending to paperwork Boris refuses to go forward when being ridden or lead. He very much mirrors the part of me that is stuck and doesn't want to move forward. Usually that is down to my fear – fear of my purpose, fear of taking the lead in some areas of my life. I don't like doing the bookwork part of the business and Boris doesn't like school work. Take him on a ride out (what we call a hack) and he loves it. Although he still doesn't want to take the lead I think that what he mirrors is the part of me that just needs to get out there and have some fun.

Case Study 5: Bosses behaving badly

One client was having problems with her bosses. Even though she kept changing jobs, some of the constant challenges she faced were: being micro-managed, being criticised and never feeling acknowledged or appreciated. We applied the Law of Reflection, which wasn't obvious in the beginning, to explore where she behaved like her boss. Where did she micro-manage others or herself, when did she criticise herself?

At the time she had a horse at livery and every day she would check with staff at that yard whether everything had been done. Without realising it, every time she went in she would find fault (remember from Chapter 1 how people assign you scripts). It beggars belief that the one water bucket out of twenty that accidently got missed would be hers. Unconsciously, she was attracting these events to prove her belief system right.

"How often do you praise yourself?" I asked her "How often do you tell yourself you have done an excellent job?" "Well, never," she said. "I always expect myself to do better. It has to be perfect."

The challenge with perfectionism is that people only focus on what is imperfect. Rather than allowing them to label themselves a perfectionist I tell them they are an 'imperfectionist'. In my world, a true perfectionist would recognise the perfection in everything. Purely semantics I know, but look at the implication.

When we identified this aspect within my friend, we looked at how to integrate it so that she could maintain her own high standards while also supporting, rather than criticising herself, whenever she came across an area for improvement. Outwardly this integration showed up by her bosses changing their attitude towards her or, in some cases, the boss either left or moved to a different part of the company.

Birds of a feather flock together

Under the Law of Attraction, people with similar scripts and belief systems gravitate towards each other. If you can choose to make a behavioural change within you, I guarantee that your boss will be different to you, even if he or she isn't towards other people.

The relationship you are experiencing echoes the relationship you have with yourself

If you continue to play with the premise that we are all one and that everyone is a reflection of an aspect of yourself it is possible to conclude that you are only ever dealing with yourself.

This means that whatever is going on in your relationship is happening in your mind, granted usually subconsciously or even unconsciously (even further from our awareness).

Everyone has exactly the same personalities within and without. How you express your individuality is through a blend of these parts of you, in your own unique mix. In other words, we all have a selfish side, a martyr side, an honest self, a dishonest self, a lazy part, workaholic part, an organiser and chaotic side. When you are expressing one side in an extreme way the Laws of Attraction and Reflection bring to you the complete opposite. Opposites attract, yet like also attracts like, (think shoals of fish or herds of horses). However, for opposites to attract the energy has to have the same essence.

If we go back to our earlier example, someone who is always in sacrifice will attract the opposite i.e. someone who is selfish. One person is serving everyone else; the other is serving no one but themselves. Neither is right nor wrong. We need both aspects. If we are only ever on one side of the pendulum we are out of balance.

It is not that we have to be exactly in the middle; rather we need to be able to move in and out of the different aspects.

- If you're always serving everyone but yourself do *you* need to learn to be a bit more selfish and allow yourself to serve you as well?
- If you're the one who is always being selfish then do *you* need to learn to think of others and serve them as well as yourself?

When you get both opposite sides working together, you have the best of both worlds. You can go the extra mile if you need to, with the knowledge and power to be able to say no to others when you have to recharge and serve your own interests.

One other important point is that when we are out of balance on one side of the pendulum we are usually operating out of compensation, fear and need.

When we allow ourselves to work in better balance, we are able to function more easily from love and compassion and understanding.

If you are in conflict with your partner or anyone, study what the *essence* of the argument is. It usually boils down to a conflict between our sub-personalities. The fascinating thing with all our sub-personalities is that each and every one believes it is doing its best for us as a whole. Most of the programming and requests to work for us in a certain way stem from childhood when we made up our minds that to behave, or not to behave in a certain way, would help us get our needs met.

What you see is what you get

Working with the horses at the HEART Centre to unearth the parts you might be hiding is fun and makes for interesting exploration.

- Boris may reflect your resistant side – the part not wanting to do things.
- Tigger is a good reflection of the way you may be able to help rekindle peoples' confidence.
- Tijor may reflect the part of you that is defensive and has not completely healed stuff from the past that has made you angry.
- Rodney is my fun, 'let's get on with life' self.
- Merlin is a mirror of one's wise self and in the herd he can't bear getting into fights or herd politics.
- Trezzy mirrored the part of me that was regularly out of control in the early days but as I calmed down and got my life into balance so did she. Miraculously, it didn't take strong bits and gadgets to do it, which in my ignorant days I had tried as a way of attempting to slow her down.

- Patch, when he was alive, was the rebel. He had a complete disregard for fences and I have to confess I am a bit of a rule breaker myself.

- Sugar, as her name suggests, mirrors the parts that act all sweetness and light but are different underneath. In the ménage she was Miss Perfect for the children but as soon as she went on a hack in the countryside, she was off – completely unstoppable. For the most part I am pretty well behaved but at times I so want to run free from responsibility.

Whenever I get a new horse into the yard I am always curious to find out which of my parts they will express.

When you love yourself you can marry anyone

As you go through life you will be given opportunities to meet lots of different aspects of personalities. Some will be quite dark in their character because they need the light of understanding shone on them. Some will be easy to find and see the roles of these facets. Some parts you may refuse to admit to being a part of you.

Appreciating and applying the Law of Reflection is an essential factor in creating compassionate relationships. Discovering your shadow selves in other people is vitally important for the achievement of successful communication between people and is at the very HEART of Stable Relationships and The Healing Power of Horses philosophy. When you come and have an experiential day with us you have the opportunity to explore all the different horses and discover which ones represent your dark horse. This then allows you to move yourself out of compensation, victimhood and back into balance.

When you are ready to explore how your dark horse may be sabotaging your relationships go to www.theheartofstablerelationships.com/bonus3 where you can download your voucher for a half price session.

Healing Power of Horses Principle 2

"If you spot it,
You have got it.
So let us horses show you
How to integrate it."
The Horses

CHAPTER 3

Hold your horses! Are you controlling your emotions? Or are your emotions controlling you?

WHERE DO EMOTIONS AND FEELINGS come from? What do emotions and feelings have to do with creating stable relationships? Why is it important to feel emotions? What effect does it have when you don't?

Emotions are energy in motion (e-motion). Feelings are a result of thinking. It is almost impossible to have an emotion or feeling without some form of thinking or judgement coming from your thoughts.

For example, the physical energy you feel when you're angry is the same energy as when you feel passionate; the energy when you feel fear is the same as when you feel excited (e.g. butterflies in your stomach). It is only what you think about the situation that determines how you label the feeling.

When you resist feeling your emotions, they don't just magically disappear they get buried alive. They carry on processing within you. The results of these unfelt emotions can be illness, relationship breakdowns, financial issues, career challenges and even car problems. Have you heard of blowing a gasket?

For the vast majority of us there is a huge fear of feeling. The general consensus is that emotions are bad, or weak or only for emotional people. Being strong isn't the same as *not* feeling. In fact, that is giving your power away to emotions. However, it's not about being hysterical either as that is also not really feeling your feelings. Some people even have the erroneous belief that they are able to control their emotions by not feeling them. The reality is that their emotions are actually controlling them.

Pushing feelings down can often lead to depression or *suppression* as I like to call it. We don't believe we have the right, the support or the strength to express what we are really feeling.

How do horses help us to express our emotions? I believe because they are such emotive beings themselves they are able to pick up on what we are feeling really easily. Horses are able to tune into the energy of emotions. Horses have to survive in the wild. They can tell whether the energy they are sensing is dangerous or safe. When you approach a horse they see your emotional energy field before they see you as a person; you become transparent. They respond instantly to the emotions you are holding in your vibration and if there is a level of incongruence between physical body language and emotional vibration, some horses will react quite demonstratively.

When horses are in the field, they know instantly what one another is feeling. When they are frustrated they show this straight away. This doesn't mean that horses are immune to feeling depressed, sad, frustrated or even shut down but it is interesting to note that when they are in captivity they end up having these feelings longer because often they have less power to change them.

If a wild horse feels frustrated about the lack of food

resources it will seek to change its location, often travelling 10-15 miles a day to remove itself from the cause of frustration. When a modern, conventionally kept horse suffers from food frustration it can't do anything about being locked in a cage-like stable. Often the rest of the horses in that stable block are also feeling resource-challenged and this is when they start exhibiting emotional stress.

Case Study 6: Angst in the Air

At my yard recently, most of the horses were picking on one another. My herd of horses is normally quiet, peaceful and playful but there was a lot of angst in the air. They definitely weren't happy about something, even to the point that one girl got nipped out of the blue as she walked past the stable, while another person was warned off by a horse raising its back legs to her. This was totally out of character for the horses.

I looked hard at the situation with the staff and on the surface things seemed ok, but as I felt into the energy I could sense something wasn't quite right. It transpired there was a lot of resentment and frustration over a new person who wasn't pulling her weight.

Instead of communicating with that person, the other staff grew more and more resentful and the whole atmosphere became charged. The horses picked up on this energy and mirrored the incongruence. We had a staff meeting to air these differences and by owning our anger and frustration the horses no longer needed to out-picture what was going on within us. Consequently, they returned to their normal, peaceful selves.

Case Study 7: Emotional Control

Trezzy was a feisty, dapple grey mare about 15h.h. She came into my life when I was pretty out of control with my emotions, money, relationships and business. Needless to say, she was the horse that was always out of control when I rode her. She perfectly mirrored me and my life. One of the hardest things my ego personality had to come to terms with was how detached and distant she was from me. (I never used to cope with rejection very well in any form.)

She triggered my desperate need to be loved and accepted, but no matter what I did she had an air of detachment and aloofness towards me. I felt I wasn't her special human. She touched all my beliefs around rejection, being unwanted and unlovable. Of course, at the time she fuelled my assumption that if a horse didn't want to be with me, what chance did I have with humans?

When I looked at the times when she didn't want to be near me, I realised it was when I was carrying more balls of emotional energy than I wanted to admit to. She would sense my unexpressed grief or my pent up frustrations and anger and literally try to get as far away from me as possible. Looking back, with the knowledge I have since gained from the horses, it wasn't the grief or anger as such but my denial of and disassociation from the emotions that she reacted to most strongly. The inauthenticity I exuded probably made her feel quite insecure around me.

What I discovered is she would only come near me when I really felt my emotions. However, I always dreaded connecting to my feelings. My fear was that if I got in touch with the hurt, anger or grief I felt those feelings would never stop.

Through the horses teaching me about feelings I discovered something really new: ; far from fearing that the feeling would never stop, the reverse was true. It is like a cloud that rains. Once that cloud has emptied itself of rain, that particular cloud cannot rain the same rain again.

It's the same with emotions: once you feel that particular layer of emotion it goes completely. Admittedly, another cloud or layer may come up to be released but at least the realisation that the emotion would stop, gave me the strength and courage to truly connect with my feelings.

Trezzy provided a perfect example of how buried emotions can affect relationships. When you carry a lot of emotional baggage people want to be as far away from you as possible.

Another interesting fact about emotions is that rather than having to release all the stored emotions one by one, if you can get to the root cause of, or belief behind them, you can bring all the other emotions down. It's like taking the bottom can off a display in the supermarket.

So how can understanding your own emotions help your relationships? One of the observations I have made is that whatever you are feeling, the other person is sensing the same. However, what can happen is that one party will tend to suppress or disassociate emotionally, while the other person will often be over expressive. Or, another common dynamic is that one person takes all the responsibility and the other does all the emotions in the relationship. Unfortunately, this is often the cause of much confrontation and unrest in communication. 'You're so cold, you never express your emotions,' is a typical accusation or: 'oh you're just being hysterical' is often a retort.

This is where working with the horses can help identify the blocked emotions or incongruence in your feelings. Because the emotions are an energy, the horses pick up on these very easily. The result of becoming congruent with your feelings and expressing them healthily is stable relationships, health to your body and flow in your finances and career.

I have had several horses that, when I have been angry at something or someone, have seen me coming and immediately got out of my space. They often put their ears back at me as a sign to not go near them with all my stuff. Like people, horses can also help bring out an emotion by acting in a certain way. My horse Tigger would often sense when I was furious about something and would deliberately play up to make me angry to release that feeling.

Case Study 8: Strong Silent Support

Sam, the Shire, is very good at supporting people dealing with a lot of emotion. One such occasion was a lady who came to overcome her fear of riding and get her confidence back.

We went into the stable to start grooming Sam. I asked a few preliminary questions about the fear and then allowed to her have some quiet time to connect with him. Not more than 10 minutes passed when she suddenly burst into floods of tears.

After allowing the space to just let the feelings flow, I softly asked what had happened. It turned out that she had experienced the most terrible tragedy in her life, losing her son in a motorbike accident and one she just couldn't and wouldn't let herself get over. She had refused all forms of counselling and talking therapies.

However, just a short space of time of being with Sam allowed several years of sadness to pour out from her. The relief she felt was tremendous and hardly a word needed to be said. His gentle authenticity provided the safe space for her to express herself and release gallons of grief. The horses were able to give a safe and sensitive space to heal.

Often when people have a fear around riding, one of the hidden dynamics can actually be a fear of feeling. Giving yourself permission to express your emotions honestly is the best healing medicine

---

When you feel it, you can heal it
Wendyism

Just like people, not all horses respond in the same way to a given situation. It is the skill of the equine therapist to be able to read the horses' reactions and to understand what is happening. With the Laws of Reflection and Attraction working, we then need to piece together who is reflecting what.

The great advantage of working with horses therapeutically is that they don't have an agenda in the way that humans do. It doesn't mean they don't have their own story too, which has made them believe certain things about life or people. However, what you come up against is a clean response.

Often people who have been abused resonate with horses that have similar backgrounds. They will form bonds that other humans and horses do not. This is again down to the Laws of Attraction and Reflection.

This can be the same when two people meet in a relationship. They will usually bring the same theme to be healed but it is often played out differently on either side. A big clue as to what is going on emotionally is to check what you're feeling. Most times that is what is happening for your partner or the other person in the relationship. Or, you may be coming up against your shadow unconscious self.

When working with humans or horses that have been abused, it is really important that there is someone with a positive influence to be able to take them both forward. We don't want to get stuck in the 'I was abused, ain't life awful' syndrome. Otherwise, we stay stuck, drowning in the well. If you're not careful it is very easy to get caught up in 'woundology' or addiction to victimhood. We then end up using our wounds to manipulate and control people, rather than healing and letting go.

Current pain can be:

- *P*ast
- *A*ctions
- *I*nvading the
- *N*ow.

Wendyism

What can you learn from horses about how to deal with emotions?

If you observe a healthy herd of horses, you will notice that their emotions are very much in the now, felt and dealt with. You won't see a horse that has been bullied by another horse sit and seethe with resentment, plotting revenge. It doesn't serve the herd to have constant fights and upsets. Being prey animals, if they were in the wild that would draw attention to them and make them vulnerable to predators. Their overall intention is to be at peace with one another. This means scuffles are quickly sorted and stability restored.

What can you take from this?

Ask yourself:

- Do I use my emotions as weapons?
- Do I attack people with my anger, even if just verbally?
- Do I use my grief to make others feel sorry for me?
- Do I hang on to resentments rather than be honest and communicate my feelings

- Do I use anger to hide my fears?
- Do I use blame of others or myself to stop myself moving forward?
- Have I camped out in my guilt, resentment grief, or other emotion?

Heal the hidden cause

You are seldom angry for the reason you think you may be. More often than not, when you're angry with others it's because you are angry with yourself for a similar or the opposite reason.

For example, a customer recently stole from me a month's livery for her horse. She literally did a moonlight flit, taking her horse off in the night without paying. I was furious with her for doing this 'to me' but what I was really angry about was the fact that I had been lazy about getting her to sign her livery agreement upfront and paying a month in advance. I had been going on holiday and thought: 'oh that will be ok'. This episode also triggered my memories of all the other events in my life where I had been caught out because I'd been less than on the ball.

Case Study 9: Magic touch

We were working with a group of vulnerable adults and this one lady "Belinda" arrived in a really aggressive mood and it was quite apparent that she didn't really want to be there.

"I hate talking and sharing in groups" she snarled.

Further angry outbursts pursued. My co-facilitators and I just non-judgementally held the space for her and allowed her time to express herself.

We progressed onto choosing a horse to work with. As she went up to each of the horses they backed off from her very angry energy. None of the horses felt safe enough to be around her

For the first time in her life, "Belinda" realised what the effect her hostile energy was having on the people around her. She was deeply hurt that none of the horses wanted to be with her, let alone work with her. To save face from the other group members, she pretended she didn't want to do the exercise and stormed out and took herself off to the back of the stables.

Unbeknown to her, she was standing next to one of the outer stables, where we put the rehabilitating horses who aren't emotionally ready for too much human interaction. As the tears gently rolled down her cheeks, Harry (one of these afore mentioned horses) lent round the end of his stable and very gently placed his muzzle by her face. As she got in touch with her authentic emotions it allowed someone to be able to connect with her. This someone just happened to be a horse.

The effect was just as extraordinary as if we had sprinkled fairy dust on her.

She was over the moon that Harry had "chosen" her. Suddenly she literally went from this antagonistic grown up child to this amazing animated adult. She insisted on working with Harry and the two of them got on together as if they had known one another all their lives.

As we discussed in Chapter 2 like attracts like. Harry too came to us in the beginning, aggressive, mistrusting of humans because of his abusive formative years and was extremely exhaustingly unco-operative. Normally he can be far too much of a horse to handle for a beginner. Belinda and Harry resonated with one another.

"Belinda" became willing, enthusiastically sharing her experiences with the exercises and even allowed herself to drop her angry defensiveness and actually start feeling happy.

I later heard she went onto volunteering to help other people with addictions.

All this - just from one day on one of our unique workshops.

Personal Anecdote: A Hidden Pay off

A while back, my husband was constantly working weekends. When I had my original riding school this didn't matter but I had recently sold it and had time on my hands. The fact that he was now busy and I wasn't caused major conflict in our relationship.

So, when he went off at weekends I processed his absence as him not wanting to be with me. And of course that fed into all my earlier childhood stuff about being unwanted and unlovable. The amount of rage I felt was totally disproportionate to what was actually happening. So, I was quite intrigued when it was suggested to me that I might be doing other peoples' emotional work, namely my husband's.

I tested this theory by pretending I had set this scenario up. Firstly, I had to look at how being so emotionally hysterical served me and through the coaching I was receiving, I discovered that this was a way to avoid authentic intimacy.

The next step was to pretend that I wanted him to work weekends. The hidden pay off was that I could actually have time to myself to do things for me. I set about not reacting angrily when my husband went off to work yet again at the weekend and I looked forward to the weekend by myself. The result was fascinating.

Firstly, when I stopped reacting angrily and stayed truly

peaceful, my husband started to come home really frustrated with other workmates and work situations. He actually started doing his own emotional work. Then, blow me down with a feather, he stopped working weekends. My 'me-time' was very short lived. Be careful what you wish for!

Healing Power of Horses Principle 3

"When you allow yourself to feel
You give yourself a chance to heal
When near us with your feelings be real
Emotions are really no big deal"
The horses

CHAPTER 4

Getting Back in the Saddle
Overcoming fears, fantasies and phobias

During my 20+ years of helping people overcome their fears around horses, I have become fascinated by the parallels between these fears and relationships. It's no coincidence that the fear of what might happen when they ride or handle their horses mirrors what they fear or feel could happen in a relationship. Indeed, my own fear of horse jumping reflected the absolute terror I was experiencing in a violent, dysfunctional relationship. However, the tools I used to overcome that terror were to become the launch pad for the amazing work with horses I am passionate about sharing.

My biggest fear about jumping was that I would never get over the jump safely to the other side. The analogy for me at that time was I could never see myself getting out of this unhealthy relationship safely and in one piece, either. If you approach a jump with so much indecision, inner conflict and lack of conviction the horse usually feels this energy and is likely to lose confidence about going over the jump or start to feel insecure about the rider, resulting in a refusal or run out.

Unconsciously, this may be happening in a relationship too. In my own situation I would often be met with either a plea from my partner not to leave him, when he was sober, or a terrorising threat, usually when drunk, of the consequences if I did. I was too afraid to leave and even more afraid to stay.

Here are a couple of other common reflections and parallels between horses, riding and relationships it might mean:

I am afraid the horse will ditch me = I am afraid he will leave me

I am afraid the horse won't like me = If I am myself in a relationship my partner won't like me

If I stand up to this horse he may get angry with me and hurt me = If I don't do what my partner wants he may find someone else who will

Other worries often have a deeper fear:

What if I get hurt (fear of rejection or abandonment)?

What if she gets to know me and doesn't like me (fear of intimacy)?

What if she has an affair (fear of betrayal)?

What if he doesn't want to have a long term partnership (fear of commitment)?

What if he isn't Mr Right (fear of making a wrong choice)?

What if they find out what I am really feeling (fear of being honest)?

What is the one thing these statements and questions have in common? They are all about the future. They are all in the "what if" category. It's amazing that with all this fear, there is any room for actual love. You cannot love and fear at the same time as it is a contradiction.

> *"Where there is so much fear,
> Love can nowhere be near."*
> **Wendyism**

Love doesn't hurt

I have often used the principle: 'If it hurts, it's not love,' as my barometer. So, if it's not love, what is it then? According to Chuck Spezzano, the eminent spiritual psychologist, it is *need*. It is the attachment to outcomes; it is the erroneous belief that says you're not worth it, you can't cope, or that you cannot live without the other person.

One of the most common fears people have around horses is of getting physically hurt. This can range from people worrying about falling off to being confined in a stable with horses.

Case Study 10: Trapped and Trampled

One lady I was working with was so terrified of being around horses that we couldn't even get into the stable. She feared she would feel trapped and not be able to get out if she needed to. She was anxious that the horse would then trample or kick her.

I asked her how those fears might translate in her relationships. As she reflected on her past and current relationships she could see she had exactly that same fear. She had been in relationships where she had felt trapped and afraid that she wouldn't be able to escape.

She had partners that had walked all over her, literally trampling her needs. She had also been in quite abusive situations.

Getting Back in the Saddle

We worked through how to overcome her fear around the horses and then explored how she might be able to use those tips and tactics to feel more secure in her relationships.

I am happy to report not only does she feel really safe around horses but she is confidently looking forward to getting married to her current partner.

How does the fear of getting hurt come about? You've probably placed your need on a particular person to behave in a certain way. You need them to follow your script about relationships e.g. they have to stay with you and if they don't follow your script then they are the bad guys. Why should they stay with you? Who started the belief that people have to stay with you? Great if they do but it really isn't the end of the world if they don't.

Looking back on my life I can honestly say I am relieved that some relationships didn't work out. Otherwise I would never have met my wonderful husband. Sometimes ladies, you have gotta kiss a lot of frogs 'til you find your prince. (Sorry gentlemen, I am not sure what the equivalent saying is).

If you are in pain or emotionally hurt, ask yourself what did you want from this particular person? There must have been an unmet need to have created that pain. You can't have loved them unconditionally. Unconditional love does not have conditions.

If a person has betrayed you, what was the script you assigned them? Was it that they had to stay faithful to you? Again it is a need. If they betrayed you, are you saying they should only be with you? Why? Who says so? Remember too, if someone is betraying you to ask yourself "how am I betraying them or how am I betraying myself?" (See Chapter2). If we label behaviour as betrayal, we are admitting a need. Did you need them to stay with you for you to feel loved or accepted? At some level all betrayal is self-betrayal.

Letting go is hard to do

One of the exercises we do at the HEART Centre involves working with horses 'at liberty' i.e. without any means of control. The goal is to find a way of being with the horse that encourages the horse to stay with you. The interesting observation about this exercise is that the greater the person's need, the less likely the horse is to want to be with them.

Cats are superb at teaching us about neediness. Have you ever noticed how cats always make a beeline for the person who doesn't want them and scarper from those who are desperate for the cat to come to them?

When you have authentic self-love you do not make prisoners of people. Why would you want someone to be with you if they weren't happy? Why would you want to keep someone in a relationship with you if they didn't want to be there - unless it is selfishly to fulfil a need in you?

The irony is that when you sincerely allow somebody to have freedom and you love that person unconditionally, in my experience they don't want to go. Why would they? They are receiving pure love. Isn't that what we all desire?

My understanding is that people only go off elsewhere when they are not receiving pure love; feel they are being eaten up by the other person's need or when they lack self-love and integrity. They may also be acting out a script or belief they or the other person has. In the wild, horses have no concept of abandonment. Boy horses don't get screwed up when mum ousts them to go and live in the bachelor herd. They have an order of life and a family unit that works and creates security. Mum and dad are around, delivering guidance and discipline in the early years and then that's it: they have to find their own way. I firmly believe they are in a natural state of love and regard for one another.

Enter humans. We whisk the foals away far too early from their mothers (in the racing industry this is as young as three months). In the wild they would be with their mother for at least 2-3 years, after naturally weaning at 9-11 months. We seldom allow sire and dam to stay with the youngsters, so they become one parent families. We can see the evidence in our own society of the struggle and stress that broken homes have on everyone. We have created separation anxiety in horses and resource fighting. This is all because of our needs: to make money, to ride the horse, to have control over horses.

What would happen if we didn't have to make money, or if we had all the time and resources? Modern horses wouldn't be so screwed up. How does this relate to our relationships? Because we operate from fear, we suffocate; we create separation anxiety in one another. "I'm afraid you're going to leave me," and "you're afraid I'm going to abandon you." We cling to one another in our neediness.

In to me see

Are you afraid of intimacy? When you love and accept yourself fully this can no longer be a fear.

Do you erroneously think that if the other person in the relationship knew that you had a particular personality trait they would run a mile? Newsflash: we all have these peculiar traits. We all have a selfish side, we all lie, cheat, steal and have murderous tendencies. If you refer back to Chapter 2 you will see that all of us have every type of personality trait within us.

Usually, we don't express our less desirable sides outwardly. However, would it be fair to say you often rob yourself of self-worth, or that you attack yourself mercilessly? How many of you kid yourselves about how you feel and lie by saying "I'm fine!" when asked? How often do you cheat yourself of self-love and respect?

Overcome your fears

First of all you have to find the need that you fear won't be met in a relationship.

One lady who came on the Healing Power of Horses course had a need for love. Over the years she had given herself a really hard time by believing she wasn't lovable. She worked with Brenbo, a stunning palomino that had been shunted from home-to-home until he came to the HEART Centre.

Due to his physical challenges, Brenbo never really did much except stand in his box, but he had an inexplicable way of melting people's hearts and giving them a taste of pure love. The lesson from Brenbo was that you only had to be yourself to be lovable. People working with him didn't have to do anything; they just needed to be themselves.

When people opened themselves to receiving without expectation, they felt this powerful little pony's love. When this lady experienced Brenbo's love for no reason other than the fact she was there, she found it hard to believe that she didn't need to earn it, deserve it or have to trade something for that love.

Think about that for a moment, do you believe that you have to earn love? Do you believe that love is something you end up deserving because you have been a good girl or boy? Do you believe you have to trade your true desires to get love? Do you believe you have to be someone you are not in order to get that love?

I think this is where working with horses is so wonderful. They don't care what you are wearing, there isn't the smell of Armonia perfume as much as there is an aroma of ammonia from the stables. They don't recognize a prince over a pauper. They just accept you for who you are.

I'm not saying you'll have this experience with all horses. Sadly, some horses have had such traumatic experiences with humans that it has robbed them of the trust they once had in us. However, even the most abused horse can have its trust restored in humans through the right methods. Several of the horses that have found their way to me had an unpleasant start.

Just because one human beat the life out of us, doesn't mean everyone else is going to do the same. Monarch, Rosie, Harry,

Smartie and I are living proof. These horses have had to change their beliefs about humans. I had to change my beliefs about what I deserved in life and from relationships. It is the only way to go from fear to love. As my little pony said "love without expectation."

So, how do we overcome our fears? Well, the first thing I teach people when they are working with any type of fear is to get it out of the future. Fear can only live in the future. Even if your horse is bolting with you in the saddle and you're feeling terrified the fear is because you are anticipating what might happen. The reality is that the horse is just going fast; the fear is it may not stop. So, your mind goes into overdrive about what may or may not happen if you can't stop.

The mind conjures up all sorts of dramas. However, if you bring your mind back to the present you go into thinking about what you might do next, instead of reacting with fear.

What do we really fear? What is fear? Where do irrational fears come from?

Fundamental fears are based on future thinking and the belief that we are going to lose something or someone. We fear not being able to control life, things, people and outcomes. We even fear that we won't be able to control our feelings.

> *"When you go into fear*
> *You go out of the present."*
> ***Wendyism***

Here is an illustration of how we attract the right horse, human or situation to bring a problem to the surface for healing.

Case Study 11: You can have it all

Barclay is a magnificent, glistening conker brown Irish thoroughbred about 16.2h.h. He is normally a very willing character, eager to please humans and uncomplicated.

On this particular day we were working on relationship beliefs and fears when one of the students, Vanessa, believed she couldn't have a wonderful relationship and also do what she wanted to career wise. Her fear was she would have to choose and that it would have to be either/or, rather than both.

As Vanessa tackled the obstacle we had assigned to her she kept going back and forth trying to make this horse do what she wanted. Every time she took a step forward and asked Barclay to follow, when he didn't respond straight away she quickly stepped back to where she had started, asking with *all* her focus still on Barclay.

Various options were explored even to the point where she tried dragging the horse to the next part of the obstacle. Barclay was having none of it. He just stayed rooted to the spot. This brought masses of other beliefs and fears up which we spent time working through.

Once we had released the emotions and explored the validity of her beliefs, Vanessa changed her limiting beliefs to what she really wanted to believe. We then invited her to get into the feeling and vibration of each belief. She identified from the coaching that she needed to keep focused on where *she* wanted to go and what *she* wanted to do.

The other challenge she needed to overcome was to let go of the anxiety over whether a particular partner would come along on her path. She was afraid that if she chose her passion and purpose, she would lose her partner. Equally if she chose her partner she dreaded just being a housewife, with no career.

Whilst some people can be very happy in that role, Vanessa wasn't quite ready for that.

Vanessa changed her beliefs, let go of her fear and instead visualised what a particular scene would look like with her partner supporting her and doing what she loved, then verbalised her new beliefs. "I now choose to have a wonderful, loving partner who supports me in my dreams and career." As she gave energy to that belief, a miraculous thing happened: Barclay, who initially had his feet firmly planted, started walking, following Vanessa without any coercion, control or confrontation.

Vanessa burst into tears of joy. The realisation that all she needed to do was focus on what she authentically wanted to do and confidently step towards that goal, actually gave her the very thing she wanted: a loving partner to share her journey with *and* a rewarding career.

Since doing this exercise, Vanessa is still with her now wonderfully supportive partner and she is doing the work she loves.

One key point to remember when working with beliefs and fears is that you're not trying to control anybody. Believing that somebody is being and doing the best they can sends out energy of love and validation. However, it's another thing to say "Johnny now allows me to work where I want." This suggests that Johnny has control over where you can or can't work. This isn't strictly true. You may give away your power to another person that allows them to control you but in truth they can't really.

On the other side of the pendulum, if you are the one objecting to what others are doing, you don't have the right to take away another's free will, although you do have the right to set appropriate boundaries. If you set boundaries, they will have to be kept. You have to be prepared to follow through with your consequence if somebody chooses to challenge that boundary with their behaviour; otherwise it just becomes a meaningless threat.

Case Study 12: Boosting Boundaries

Janet was very worried about going into the stables with the horses. She had a big fear that the horses would bite, kick or crush her. I invited her to explore how this might be a metaphor for her relationships. She recognised that this was a big fear she had in relationships too. When she was in a relationship instead of enjoying it, she realised that she spent more of her energy worrying about how they might hurt her in some way.

She chose Smartie to work with but every time he challenged her, she would back off or try and appease him. Instead of centering herself and taking the lead, she allowed herself to be continually pushed around by him. Their partnership deteriorated rapidly. I enquired why she was unable to set any personal boundaries with him.

It turned out she was afraid to in case Smartie wouldn't like her or that he might get angry with her. She then feared she would get rejected or hurt in some way. I asked if she was scared to set boundaries in her relationships for the same reason. Naturally she had the same pattern.

As we progressed with the session, Janet and Smartie's partnership continued to deteriorate further. I invited Janet to start valuing herself and set appropriate boundaries.

"No" had to mean "no". She had to overcome her fear that if she stood up for herself he wouldn't like her. I posed the question "Did she really believe Smartie liked and respected her anyway?

Janet found the courage to start setting clear and fair boundaries with Smartie. He tried it on a couple of times but Janet continued to follow through with her boundaries. When she changed her belief, as well as her actions, Smartie settled down quite quickly.

Janet became aware that actually boundaries made Smartie much happier to be around her. She realised far from disliking her, their relationship really improved.

When you value and respect yourself more fully, under the Law of Attraction you are likely to attract a much higher vibration of partnership to you.

FEAR

> Future
> Experience
> Anticipated
> Real

Your mind has a very powerful imagination and with your fear comes an elaborate fantasy. When your mind runs away with your thoughts anything can happen.

Would it be fair to guess that when you start feeling fear your mind begins to create catastrophes? Does your mind always leap to the worst case scenario? Well that's ok. Initially, remember your fear response is there to keep you safe. However, what is common is to only play the disaster movie up until the point of the tragedy and stop there.

Once your mind has a picture of a story ending in a certain way, it creates a feeling, usually pain of loss, hurt, stress etc. Remember your mind relates to these pictures as if they were real. In the memory part of your mind there isn't a past or future. There is only the now. Your chatterbox mind says: "better not do that then as you will end up feeling awful," because it is feeling the end of the story in this very moment.

When I work with my clients around riding or horse fears, I encourage them to take their disaster movie further by playing the "So what then?" game. I then invite them to go beyond the disaster. What usually comes out from this exercise is revealing.

Exercise 3: So What Then?

I would like you to think of the worst case scenario regarding the relationship you are working with for this exercise.

You may dread your partner leaving you.

So what then? (Your answer)

And if that happens, so what then? (Your answer)

And if that happens, so what then? (Your answer)

Keep repeating this question until you get to the point of realising that actually you would survive, find peace and be able to get on with your life.

One of the most irritating and useless bits of so-called advice I hear people being given is "don't show the horse you're afraid". The horse knows, smells and can identify your fear, even before you have gone up to him/her. Their ability to read the auric energetic field of other animals (especially predators) is what has kept them alive for millions of years. So reading yours is no different. What alarms them is incongruence: your energetic field is saying one thing, your physical body another and your mixed message thinking (which they pick up as well) adds to the pool of inauthenticity.

I teach people to be honest about their feelings and to imagine they can talk to the horse and share them. Whenever one lady I worked with went up to Harry he would turn round and try and bite or kick her, which obviously fuelled her fear. When I suggested she tell Harry exactly how she felt when he behaved like this, she was utterly gobsmacked at how he allowed her into his stable.

The truth was that both horse and human were connecting through their vulnerabilities. Harry, because of his earlier years of abuse, was very protective of his space when new people arrived. The lady had a very similar issue.

When I suggested she applied the same principle to her home life and relationships, she could see the parallels. She went home and gently explained to her partner how she was really feeling. This resulted in a greater connection between them and created much more stability.

Often we project our stuff onto the other person: a behaviour, a belief or an emotion that we have. They have no option but to respond in less than positive ways in their actions to these projections.

In the herd, horses are much more authentic with their emotions and feelings and tend, for the most part, to deal with their stuff straight away. Although they live by their instincts, if they start to feel anxious or afraid they immediately deal with it through fight, flight or freeze. They don't normally hang around or make a long drama of it.

Healing Power of Horses Principle 4:

"Use your fear to keep you safe, like a friend
But don't let it take you over in the end.
When you fall off that "horse"
Just get right back on, of course."
Wendyism

CHAPTER 5

Straight from the horse's mouth Non-Verbal Communication is the loudest

We often have a fantasy in our head about what the other person is saying, thinking or doing. We also have a fantasy about how a relationship should be. The personality ego makes up stories that often keep us fearful, separate or lead to a fight.

When communication is done from the heart, both parties can reach a peaceful solution, even if sometimes in that peace there may be sadness, or not necessarily agreement. When communication comes from fear or anger- based energy, it presents either as a demand, or the other party doesn't feel there is a win-win situation.

Consider the differences in energy between a demand and a request.

    a.   "I want you to put the bin out"

or

    b.   "Would you be willing to put the bin out please?"

How would you react to each question? What feelings might you have in response to a) compared with b)?

To effectively make a request doesn't mean you have to be passive or lack authority. When a request is made with confidence and the amount of assertiveness is appropriate to the request, this instils confidence in the communication.

Here are my acronyms for demands and requests:

Destroys, destructs, dis-empowers
Emotive
Makes the other party feel taken from/wrong
Attacks
Need based
Distances, creates despondency, depresses
Separates people

Reassures, respects
Empathises, empowers
Questions if they would be willing
Unconditional, non-judgemental, unifies
Energises, equalises
Says what they mean, allows it to be ok to say no
Truthful, timely
Stabilises relationships

Non-verbal communication is 87% of all language

Studies show that non-verbal communication accounts for nearly 90% of our communication. This means that only 10% of communication is spoken word. Horses are 99% non-verbal, when you work with them to improve your own communication, you can see and feel the effect of your own non-verbal energy immediately.

Non-verbal communication is the loudest

If you watch a horse's subtle body language often you can see exactly when he/she has been asked too loudly, strongly, demandingly, thoughtlessly or confusingly. Some of the ways they protest include a swish of the tail, a grind of their teeth, a buck, a rear, bolting or planting their feet. Sometimes the body language isn't as loud as a kick but more subtle, like their ears going back or their nostrils wrinkling.

If you get a chance, watch a herd of horses communicating with one another and you will observe just how little it takes to get their messages across. You will notice that they start with the smallest of signals and progress to a bigger, more demonstrative expression. They can give at least 30 body language signals within a few seconds from a look to a kick!

I personally feel that humans have a lot to learn from their behaviour. How often do you go in all guns blazing, when actually the tone of 'pass the pepper pot please' might have had better results?

Lack of communication causes separation

When we fail to communicate effectively people build up fantasies about what we're thinking. Have you noticed that when you don't communicate with yourself properly you find yourself mired in your own conflict? Signs that this is happening include oscillating from one decision to another, being in conflict with others or feeling pulled in opposite directions.

Case Study 13:
Say what you mean, mean what you say

Tigger is a beautiful 15h.h. Connemara gelding. His presence is awe inspiring and he has got hundreds of people back in the saddle over the years. Whilst he is an amazing confidence giver, he also encourages people to be very clear in their communication.

Audrey was trying to get her children to listen to her. She was forever on their case, nagging them to clean their room, get ready for school, do their homework etc. She shared that she frequently threatened them with losing their privileges, like their iPod or play dates. However, she confessed that she never followed her threats through.

Audrey worked with Tigger. Her goal was to get him to do a specific exercise. However, Tigger is the type of horse that, if you ask him to do something without any real authority, ensures his personal desires override yours, especially if there is a nice juicy bit of grass to be eaten. Not surprisingly, he completely ignored Audrey.

Audrey was coached in how to communicate more effectively: with clarity, assertiveness and intention. As she worked with Tigger in her 'new' energy, he toddled along quite happily to the obstacle. Because Tigger was clear in his communication, Audrey went home with a new found confidence in her communication skills and, to her amazement, they worked on her children.

Think about the people you know. Who instils confidence in you? Is it the person who is wishy-washy in the way they talk or act or someone who has very clear boundaries and authority?

Stay with your feelings

When you take responsibility for how you feel about something or someone it empowers everyone around. When you say accusatory things like "you hurt me, you made me feel...." not only are you giving your power away but also *you* are now attacking the other person.

You don't know for sure that this person intended to hurt you. It was your reaction to what they did or said that caused you to feel a certain way. Only you are in control of your responses. Only you are in control of your feelings. *No one has the power to make you feel anything.*

Honesty is the best policy

Being honest is often the scariest thing to be. Either you don't want to admit to yourself what you are really feeling or you may be afraid to express your truth because of how the other person might react.

Case Study 14: Attack causes defence

Jenna was having difficulty communicating with her husband. She felt he never supported her and was really angry with him. She was invited to choose a horse that represented her husband. She chose Tijor, TJ for short, a very big ex-show jumper horse, with an even bigger presence. As she went into the stable TJ turned his back on her, causing Jenna to feel frightened and back off.

"This is just what James does." "When I try and have a conversation with him he just ignores me, or he feels too intimidating to approach". TJ continued to stay there, his bottom to her and head as far away as possible.

Still standing in the stable, we explored first of all what was going on emotionally for Jenna. She realised she felt quite angry and frustrated about things in her own life. When her husband acted the way he did this compounded her feelings and felt even more fear and frustration.

We worked on Jenna taking responsibility for what was

happening in her life and Jenna came up with a positive action plan, to make some changes.

At this point Tijor started to turn round towards Jenna.

We then discussed what she actually needed from her husband to help her feel more supported.

I invited her to have an imaginary conversation with her husband by talking to Tijor.

This time she didn't converse with attack and anger, however she did explain how his actions brought up feelings of fear and frustration in her. She asked if he would be willing to consider her request for more support around the house and be more communicative.

With that TJ came over to Jenna and put his head by her. Jenna was awestruck.

What transpired after that conversation was pretty amazing too. Jenna and James managed to have an honest discussion and it emerged that James had been feeling pretty much the same way as Jenna. He had avoided talking to Jenna as he believed he would be attacked for not getting things right in their relationship.

"When you make it true for you,
You make it true for everyone else too"
Wendyism

Empathy and compassion

When you judge another person from your map and perception of reality, you may miss a really good understanding of why people are behaving the way they are. Often when I take people round the stables and share some of the stories of the horses' backgrounds, they instantly get why that horse might be a bit nippy, protective of its space, not want to participate etc.

So, why is it so much more difficult to have that same level of empathy and compassion for another human being? "He should know better" is a common statement. Why? Why should somebody know better and if he/she did, don't you think they would have acted differently?

It's hard to accept that, at any given moment, we are all doing the best we can, particularly if an action is abusive, horrific or beyond belief. When we know that a horse or animal has been in pain we understand why it might want to lash out in some way. Nobody who communicates from the heart and with love would act in such a way. This doesn't mean to say that we should condone their behaviour but we shouldn't attack and judge without knowing the full story.

HEART to HEART

When communication is done from the heart everyone wins. Let go of the outcome needing to be a certain way. Take a risk. True communication often involves taking a risk about having a difficult conversation. Trust that whatever happens will be the highest good for all.

Healing Power of Horses Principle 5

"If you say what you mean, mean what you say
Then with us and all, you'll have a good day."
The horses.

CHAPTER 6

Wild Horses couldn't drag me away . . . Healing the heart of childhood challenges

THE SOURCE OF NEARLY ALL our present day challenges and emotions can be traced back to beliefs, assumptions and situations we either created or experienced in our formative years. When certain things have happened to us in the past often in our present day lives we attract particular scenarios that replicate these events. This tends to happen if we would have liked something to have ended differently.

Case Study 15: The Invisible Lady

One lady, who came to see me, worked with a horse that was indifferent to her. She tried various ways to persuade the horse to do what she wanted but none of the appeasement or cajoling worked. She became quite upset and assumed the belief that the horse didn't like her.

"If this was an analogy, who and what does it remind you of?" I enquired.

"My father" she replied. "When he came home from work he was always indifferent to me."

"How does that play out now in your current relationships?"

"Both my boss and partner are completely indifferent to me, too."

"How do you try and get noticed?"

"I keep doing things for them hoping they will like or notice me."

"Does it work?"

"Not really. I might as well not be there,"

"On a scale of 1-100, how much do you believe you are worth noticing and being valued?"

"Not much - about 10"

"That is what is coming across to your horse, your boss and your partner

The reality is you have no control over whether someone likes you, values you or even speaks to you. However, what you do have control over is your response, your emotions and how much you actually like, value and talk kindly to yourself.

Unconsciously, the 'invisible lady' was trying to change the way her father had acted towards her, by getting people in her presence to notice her.

If you go back to Chapters 1 and 2 you can see that people respond to you according to your belief system. Also you are subject to the Laws of Attraction and Reflection, so you attract people and situations that mirror your beliefs.

In this situation the lady had assumed that her dad's indifference to her was because she was not worth talking to. She felt that her dad didn't love her or even like her and took his behaviour personally. The chances are we have probably done something similar too.

Exercise 4: Partner or parent?

Just for fun, think of the partner you have now or had in the past.

Which traits of your parents are or were in them? They may even be similar in a physical way.

Do they have the same outlook on life?

Do they treat you in a similar way?

Or, a common current outplay in relationships is to try and get a need, which your parents were unable to fulfil, met by a partner.

Case Study 16: Abandoning the belief

When Ray came to me, he had an issue with co-dependency in relationships. He was always very needy and feared his partner might go off with another man. This was because his mother went off when he was quite young, hence his fear of abandonment.

When he first approached the horse Leah, she backed off from him. This quite upset him. I explained that because he had such neediness in his energy field it actually caused Leah to run away. The interesting thing to note is that he wasn't even all over the horse physically, just that his smothering energy was causing Leah to move away.

We then proceeded to the arena and set up some exercises with Leah. One of the exercises was to get Leah from one obstacle to the next without holding her. As Ray attempted this Leah kept going off, which was what he feared. When we explored the inference for him about her behaviour, he explained that this kept happening in his relationships too. He then became needier as each relationship came into his life. Hence his co-dependence.

Gradually, Ray was able to see the link with his past: he was trying to change the ending of the story about his mother leaving him in his current relationships. We explored how to let go of a past event, change the belief and assumption and then release his neediness in his current relationship.

We repeated the exercise but this time Ray was invited to get into the feeling and energy of: 'it's ok if Leah stays and it's ok for Leah to go'. Although initially this was a challenge, he gave Leah permission to leave if she wanted to.

As Ray restarted the exercise, Leah did begin to wander off. As we worked on Ray understanding that this action did not mean he was unlovable, rather that Leah had her own agenda, he relaxed and focused on giving himself love and attention. With that, Leah started meandering back towards him. Unfortunately, Ray got too excited and she wondered off again as she unconsciously felt his need.

Ray then got into the energy state again of: 'it's ok if she comes; it's ok if she goes.' The more Ray detached himself from the outcome, the more Leah advanced towards him.

Ray understood that trying to change the present to rectify the past was never going to work. He came to the realisation that neediness repels and detachment, which is different from indifference, attracts.

Have you ever noticed something similar in your own life?

You can have it when you don't need it

Money is a really good demonstration of this principle. When you have plenty of money coming in, more seems to flow. Frustratingly, when you start needing money, it does exactly what Leah did; it goes in the opposite direction. Add the fear of lack to the equation and it can be like watching your money disappear through a colander.

Take a moment to explore all the things you feel you really need, whether that is something practical like money, a job, a relationship or something intangible like love, affection or time. Ask yourself: on a scale of 1-10 (10 being the greatest need): how much do I believe I need this to feel, happy, safe, secure, loved etc.? Just notice if the score is at the higher end and how elusive what you want is. To change this neediness you have to find a way to let go and get into a detached state of mind. This can feel quite a leap of faith initially but what have you got to lose? If you have already being unable to receive what you want through attachment and need, then surely this is worth doing differently?

When I have worked on this principle with businesses and sales people, they have seen that when they are desperate for clients and sales they repel customers. As soon as they become detached from numbers and allow themselves to get back into the reason *why* they are doing what they are and become truer to themselves, their business and sales increase.

> *"Some things won't change*
> *Unless you change some things."*
> ***Wendyism***

Case Study 17: Typical Tactics

I went to see one lady at the livery yard where she had a horse that kept attracting different illnesses. She had chopped and changed dozens of livery yards but couldn't find a yard that she trusted to look after her horse. She always felt as though nobody paid attention to what she needed.

The 'listening' problem also manifested itself at work and in her relationships. Nobody there seemed to take notice of her needs or wishes, either. This resulted in her feeling unsupported and as though she had to do everything herself because she couldn't trust anyone to follow through.

When I suggested this might be a secret strategy she learnt as a child to justify her going into independence she stared at me in disbelief. However, as she pondered this possibility she realised how she might unconsciously be assigning people scripts to let her down.

This would then prove her beliefs right and keep her in independence. The only downside of this strategy is that it is very lonely, exhausting and doesn't allow true partnership to develop. She was certainly not going to get her or her horse's needs met with this tactic

---

Healing Power of Horses: Principle 6

"Problems will stay
Unless you love them away."
Wendyism

CHAPTER 7

Get down off your high horse! Do you want to be right or happy?

Back in medieval days, being on a high horse gave power to soldiers and political leaders and was used to intimidate the underlings and enemy soldiers on foot. Today it tends to mean that someone is acting 'all high and mighty'.

Often in relationships we get on our high horse, believing our way is the right way and we start acting out of righteous indignation. What if it turns out you are the one in the wrong? It is often said pride comes before a fall and when you're on a high horse to start with it is much further to fall.

Having studied herds of horses for many years, I've noticed that they don't get caught up in the human behaviour of having to be right about something. 'It's the principle of the matter,' is not a characteristic of the herd. Admittedly they do get caught up in the odd tiff but usually that is only when resources are limited.

I love the quote from Neale Donald Walsh's book *Conver-*

sations with God: 'What if everything you thought was right was wrong, and what if everything you thought was wrong was right?' How do you know if you are being self-caring or self-righteous? One way is to ask yourself: "Am l at peace?" Has the communication separated you from the other person energetically? Or, has there been a sense of joining (although that doesn't mean you have to agree with the other person)?

Case Study 18: Toxic Tone

Mary came into the yard and asked whether her horse had had its medicine. However, instead of hearing that as an innocent question, the staff member heard it as an attack on her ability and her not doing her job properly. This wasn't Mary's intention. The staff member mounted her high horse and proceeded to express herself angrily, going on about her boundaries and then in started accusing Mary of all sorts of things.

Mary, completely confused by the verbal attack, also defended herself. It didn't take long for an all-out war of words to break out. The outcome was two unhappy, angry people going round to other people trying to get them to join sides in their rightness and argument.

The horse not only had to deal with its own stuff but also its owner's. Due to the toxicity of the argument the whole herd at the stables was affected. There was no peace or harmony for anyone. This is such a common occurrence in families, work environments and other equestrian yards.

Animals, especially horses, are finely tuned to energies around them. Never underestimate the effect *your* energy has on your pet, your family or your environment. Animals, like children, in your custodianship take on board your emotional stuff. Unfortunately, this can have quite a detrimental effect on them.

Secret Sabateur to a Personal Anecdote

On my journey of learning the art of being an employer I once allowed a situation to arise that was quite dysfunctional. I allowed my own desperate need for a break in responsibility to cloud my judgement about hiring a particular person. She was clever about how she had set herself up on paper and when she had volunteered her services. However, as soon as she took over the position as full-time paid employee she changed completely.

I realised I had not set clear boundaries and even allowed myself to lose my position of authority. The situation with staffing was horrendous. There were screaming matches across the stables and my precious, peaceful yard had become a warzone.

As I mentioned earlier, animals get affected by the emotional energy of an environment. At the time, we had about 30 horses, 28 of whom were on the veterinary list for something or other. We normally only have about 34 maximum.

This unhealthy human situation was proving toxic to the horses' health, the health of the business, which was also impacting on clients and business, and to the health of the people caught up in it. Several staff also went off sick.

How did I resolve the situation?

Firstly, I took responsibility for my own actions, acknowledging that somewhere, somehow deep in my consciousness I had chosen this situation for a reason. It's sometimes hard for us to accept that we choose everything, albeit in a split second and then bury it deeply in our subconscious. However, I find this an empowering principle, which keeps me from being a victim in, or of life.

Another guiding principle for me is that when we are caught up in outer conflicts, they represent a deep, inner conflict. I was in conflict with the direction the business was heading in. I was literally in two minds.

The next principle I applied was to ask myself who or what this person was reflecting? Which part of me was this? (See Chapter 2). The dark horse that she was outplaying was my own saboteur. My self-sabotage sub-personality has run riot in my life several times. It often comes out when I have a new level of self-worth to integrate or an old wound or belief to heal. I spent some time healing this and the next step was to apply the principle of commitment (See Chapter 8). This person was in my life for a reason. So, energetically I committed to her. I know that sounds really strange but I had to trust the process. That meant I just sent positive loving energy to her and inwardly asked my Higher Self for the truth of the situation to be shown.

The next day, out of nowhere and over nothing, she created an argument with me. I could have chosen to become indignant and get on my high horse in self-defence. As an employer I had every right to do so. However, I chose to let her have a rant, while quietly holding my nerve and boundaries. She was quite a scary energy to be around. With that she stormed off saying "I quit."

My behaviour had proved the Law of Commitment: when you commit, if it's not true it will fall away and what is true will remain. The staffing situation quickly resolved itself and within a short while we had peace, harmony and enthusiasm again. It wasn't long before my yard of sick horses all 'magically' got well.

On my Healing Power of Horses workshops I give the students an exercise which requires them to say what they can see from where they are standing. Even though we are all in exactly the same circle, each answer is different. The people who are side-by-side may have similar views but everyone notices something different. Your map of the world is your map. It is no one else's. No one has been on exactly the same journey as you. So what right do you have to insist that yours is the right map or path? By all means share your thoughts, opinions and ideas. Allowing others the courtesy to have theirs actually creates more union. As humans we have been blessed with the gift of choice. When you extend that gift to others to choose whether they take on board your ideas you will find harmony ensues.

Also, remember in discussions to consider the earlier question: "what if everything you thought was right was wrong and what you thought was wrong was right?" It is a truly powerful place to come from and not only allows greater expansion of the mind but provides greater peace.

Case Study 19:
When you are in control you don't need to be

I can remember riding a horse called Twinkle who was galloping out of control around a cross country course. The more I fought for control of her the faster she went. I was definitely not in control. In the end, out of sheer exhaustion, I threw the reins away, accepting my impending fate of not being able to stop and – with my mind creating disaster dramas of ending up in hospital or dead. A bizarre thing happened. Twinkle immediately slowed down and came back to a walk. As soon as I stopped the fight for control she gave control back to me.

Have you ever been prepared to have to fight your corner only to be taken back by the other person saying: "yes you're absolutely right and what do you want me to do about it?" Have you noticed how this completely takes the wind out of your sails and diffuses the energy?

Of course there will be situations where you do have to set and stick to your boundaries, be in control or even stand up for what you believe in. However, if your overriding energy is to choose peace over principle then the right course of action will come about.

Exercise 5: Do you want to be right or happy?

Think about the relationship you want to transform:

How controlling are you being?

How do you insist that your way is the right way?

What if you might be wrong? What implication would that have?

If you are in an argument at the moment, how important is it really that you are right?

If you know that to be true, what would happen if you just let it go?

How would you feel allowing the other person to be right in their opinion? If it is not peaceful then you probably need some deeper healing around the situation.

What if the other person is controlling you? Decide if boundaries are actually being crossed. If not and you seemingly gave away your control to them but not your power, what difference would it make to the relationship?

Remember the more controlling a person is, the more fearful they are. They have probably been in a very vulnerable situation in the past that made them feel so out of control that they vowed never to let go again in life. Another reason for the need to be in control comes from a deep sense of loss or old heartbreak.

Case Study 20: Trying to control the uncontrollable

One client I was called to see had so much deep down fear of loss that she had become mentally paralysed about riding her horse beyond the safety of the stable-yard where she kept him. The thought that she might have an accident or that her horse would get hurt by a car or, worse still, have to be put down, was unbearable. This meant she never rode beyond the safety of the riding arena, which was very boring for her and the horse.

On the day that we tackled this fear, she confessed that she was so desperate to be in control that she had thought about stealing some road block signs and putting them up the road to divert the cars!

Some people may describe these fears as irrational. I don't because to a particular part of the mind or personality they are completely rational. However, in one of the healing techniques I used we uncovered an unresolved loss from her past.

As she gained the courage, literally stride-by-stride, to slowly let go of control and trust the outcome, we managed to successfully get up the road on her horse and back without incident.

I would love to be able to wave a magic wand and say that nothing bad is ever going to happen to you but the reality is that we live in a world of possibilities and probabilities. While it is true that you have the ability to choose and co-create, your soul is also at work so you sometimes attract events for you to grow or heal. The challenge is to see the bigger picture.

A far more effective way to deal with fear is to draw on the strong part within you that, no matter what happens, helps you to cope. I also believe that:

> **'The task before you is never greater than the Power behind you'.**
> **Ralph Waldo Emerson**

The belief that you are in charge of your life and that whatever happens you will cope, provides a sense of calm. By agreeing to work with what life deals you, rather than fighting it you will always lose when you fight reality you can gain control without really needing to.

Exercise 6: Happiness is ....

Exactly how do you define happiness in your relationships? Can you only be happy if your partner is doing what you say? Is your happiness dependent on their approval or acceptance?

Are you only happy when you are in credit and have money coming in?

Are you only happy if life is going your way?

Take a moment to do this exercise

The things that would make me happy are...................................

I would be happy if..

If it wasn't for ....I could be happy

I am afraid to be happy because..

Are there conditions on your happiness?

Do you believe you have a right to be happy?

Do you need to get off your high horse about something?

What do you feel "right" about in your relationships?

What do you feel your partner or other person in the relationship is doing wrong?

Is it a question of my way or the highway?

Conflict comes about when two or more parties think they are right and the other is wrong. They have the correct answer and the other party doesn't. What if everyone was right and everyone was wrong? Or what if nobody was right or wrong? How would that change things for you and your discussions and arguments?

If you had a discussion with somebody and they swore blind that 2+2 was 5, would you argue until you were red in the face and they believed you that it was 4? Or, is your peace of mind and happiness worth more than labouring a point? If you know in your world that 2+2=4 why waste your energy trying to convert someone else's thinking unless you're a maths teacher?

> **"For those that believe, no proof is necessary.
> For those that don't, no proof is enough."**
> **Stuart Chase, US author**

If you're having an argument do you keep going until the bitter end when the other person agrees with your opinion? You might get to be right but are they at peace? Are you at peace or just satisfied you won? This isn't about not having an opinion or sticking up for what you believe is right. What we're looking at is whether you have a pattern of always having to be in control and right about everything. At one stage in my life I had such an abusive partner that I lived in fear every day for my life until I realised it was the same terror I experienced in myself in other parts of my life. Through his behaviour I was compelled to find a spiritual way to overcome fear and deal with even the most abusive person and terrorising ordeal. Those findings became the core of my Holistic Riding work and have put hundreds of people back in the saddle by overcoming their fear of not only riding but bigger fears in their lives too.

So was my partner right or wrong to behave in that way? My personal belief is he had every right to live his life the way he chose. Controversially, I believe I had no right to insist or demand that he changed, stopped drinking or stopped beating me up. I only had the right to share my feelings and need for love and respect in a relationship and how that should look in my model of the world. He was then given a choice.

I needed to be in a relationship that reflected my new self-honouring and self-loving part. I wanted to be in a relationship where there was mutual respect. If his choice was to stay drinking and exert his rage on the world, that was fine but he could no longer be with me. (Incidentally it is not good karma to allow someone to continue to abuse another person). It was setting a loving boundary that allowed freedom on both sides.

Setting and maintaining this boundary was difficult for me at first. To break my own pattern of self-attack and abuse and actually reject someone else was challenging. However, I kept doing the releasing with love end within a short space of time I was able to unhook myself from my self-destruct pattern. Shortly afterwards my new partner showed up, reflecting that new part of me and my herd of horses returned to a state of calm.

My happiness wasn't caught up in whether or not my ex-partner stopped drinking or acting the way he did. If it had been, I would still be waiting for him to change 20 years later.

I still send my ex-partner lots of love and gratitude energetically. It is an unconditional love but unconditional love doesn't mean I should have stayed with him. Miraculously, he is still alive even though his inner torture and drinking continue. I cannot profess to understand his life path but I do know that when my life path crossed his it helped me turn everything around in my life. The experience led me to the horses and the thousands of clients I have since been able to support because of the path I was forced to find. For that I am eternally grateful to him.

I remember riding down Long Reach (fascinatingly where I ended up living and having my Holistic Horse and Pony Centre) with a client about 20 years ago and saying to her that happiness is not needing anyone or anything to make you happy. Happiness is something that comes from within.

But how can we be happy when we can't seemingly control our health or finances? How can we be happy when we can't control what the other person is doing? How can we be happy if we can't control whether someone stays with us or abandons us? How can we be happy if we can't control our employees or make our boss give us respect and a pay rise?

Do you have a need to be right all the time? What does 'do you want to be right or happy?' mean?

Let us go back to Chapter 1. your experiences of relationships and life are what you believe them to be. We discussed that whatever you believe, your mind will prove you right. So when you have a fear or belief that your partner may reject or abandon you, your mind sets about proving you right.

What if you could be happy whether your partner stayed with you or not? How would that change things? What if you believed that if you lost your job you would lose your home because there wouldn't be enough money to pay for it? Do you want to be right about that belief? Could you be happy even if you did lose your job and home? If the answer is no, then at some level you are still using your home and your job as a source of happiness. You have become attached to your props in the play of life.

When you ride horses or work with them the key is to keep them wanting to please and be willing. I believe that is a good strategy for us humans too. Interestingly, when horses have violent outbursts it is usually because they have not been heard. They are not born with rage or violence. Or, if they are, there could be a life path issue going on.

This is outside the remit of this book but if you want to know more please email: wendy@theheartofstablerelationships.com

By the time a horse kicks it has given out approximately 30 body language signals, albeit in a matter of seconds. Very rarely does a horse just kick. The lead up to this is often so quick that humans can't track all the signals. A similar scenario comes into play for humans, albeit over a longer period, when we snap because of 'the straw that broke the camel's back'.

The same process for horses begins when he/she experiences pain from the rider or being ridden (it might be pain in its own body or pain from the way it is being ridden). The horse starts to become resistant and the rider uses whips or spurs to tell the horse to get on with it. The horse continues to feel pain but resentfully continues. In the stable the horse then runs away from the saddle or becomes aggressive when the saddle goes on. It now associates the saddle with pain. Still the horse is ridden and told to get on with it. However, when someone comes in with a grooming box the horse starts to make the following associations:

Grooming = saddle = being ridden = pain.

The horse becomes defensive and starts acting aggressively. Still the rider tells the horse to get on with it, often giving it a slap. When someone enters the box they are attacked.

Human = grooming = saddle = ridden = pain.

The horse then gets labelled a 'badun' and is either sent to a 'professional' for its behaviour to be sorted (more whips, spurs and other abusive methods to show who is boss) or is headed for the knacker's yard.

By the time most horses admit they are in pain they are quite a long way down the path I've just described. Horses in the wild do not like drawing attention to them and so anyone not acting harmoniously is chased out of the herd.

It is so easy to miss the whispers

When we ignore the whispers in life, we end up with sledgehammer guidance. Has that ever happened to you?

I remember just before I got M.E., I was working over 90 hours a week. I had a day job that started at 10 a.m. and then worked in a casino until 4 a.m. I ran a livery yard, looking after my own and other people's horses. My motto back then was: 'I haven't got a moment to live because I'm living every moment.'

This would probably have been ok if I had balanced work with rest and play and dealt with the feelings I was trying to avoid. I started to tire slightly but continued to work. I broke my foot and carried on working. I got a speeding ticket and continued to work at full throttle. I was ignoring the signals from my body and life. I was feeling more and more tired but convinced I just needed a pick me-up.

I went to the doctor for a tonic but he advised me to take time off. So, what did I do? You guessed it: I continued to work! Interestingly, on my last day at work before being off with M.E. my boyfriend and I had loaded my horsebox with manure, which somebody wanted for topsoil. As we drove onto the motorway, four not just one tyres on my horsebox blew. I was literally having to deal with a load of sh*t and was 'tyred'. I was off work for over a year with M.E.

At this point, I was tested as to whether I could be happy with whatever life threw at me. My answer was definitely no. I had a tantrum with my body and life. I was defiant that I wouldn't allow this illness to get the better of me. I fought it. I certainly wasn't happy. After all, how could I be happy with an illness that made me unhappy, stopped me from working, robbed me of my life plus a host of other things that I was indignant about? I didn't have the energy for my horses, partner, friends or family. I was going to prove myself right that I could get over this (which in itself wasn't right or wrong) but it was done with the energy of fight and my need to be right.

About six months in and I was getting worse, becoming angrier and more and more miserable. To a workaholic, taking away energy was the worst possible experience and I certainly wasn't happy. Fearing that I wouldn't be able to carry on with life, I revisited my doctor, who coincidentally had lost his daughter to M.E. when she stepped onto a railway line in her confused state. I always remember him saying: "Wendy, stop fighting it. Make it your friend."

I threw the biggest tantrum and became angry with my illness, the doctor and life. I can't remember how long I spent in this tantrum but I do remember that I couldn't get the doctor's comment out of my head. Eventually, I conceded. At the time M.E. was considered to be incurable. I have since come to realise that it is curable from within i.e. in-curable.

I decided to get off my high horse and chose to explore the idea of making M.E. my friend. "Well, if you're going to be with me for life I suppose I'd better get to know you." For six months I had fought my illness and now I was learning to love it and view M.E. as trying to help me. What was it trying to do for me? Instead of moaning about everything I couldn't do I started looking at what I could do. Instead of focusing on the negative I looked at the positive. Instead of my need to be right I let go and allowed the doctor to be right. I learnt to be happy and grateful to my ME (which I definitely am).

Within six months I had made a full recovery. Not to the degree of working 90 hours a week but I got the message that I needed to reorganise my life. I learned to be happy with my M.E. (For more on recovering from M.E. read The Chrysalis Effect and Elaine Wilkins's book *'Finding M.E.'*). My M.E. not only changed my life, it saved it, too.

Exercise 7: Need to be right

Think about your relationships. Where are you demanding that people act in a certain way so that you can be happy?

Do you have a need to be right?

What if you were wrong and the other person was right?

However, if you are someone who gives your power away and always make everyone right except for yourself, can you change that round?

In arguments, do you refuse to say sorry?

Just explore and then decide if you need to be right more than at peace.

> *"Happiness is....... not needing anyone or anything to make you so."*
>
> **Wendyism**

Riding horses can create a discussion between horse and rider. The horse may want to go one way, while you want to go the other. What the horse reveals is your level of intention, commitment and body language. You may be asking your horse to go left but your body may be influencing it to go right. Or, you may think you want to go right but because there is no real intention or commitment the horse decides to go where he/she wants to instead.

One course of action to remedy this is to stay absolutely committed to the direction you wish to go in, with the whole of your mind, body and emotions. It's important not to get angry because the horse is arguing that he wants to go a different way; you stay focused on the outcome you desire. You stay looking and, where physically possible, keep your body pointed in the direction you wish to head, regardless of what the horse is doing. This is a wonderful exercise in determining how committed you are to your goal. No matter what the horse is doing, you patiently persist on your path. This is not about excessive force, in fact quite the opposite. As soon as the horse even starts to yield to the direction you wish to go in, you release the cue you have used and reward the attempt.

Another option is to go with the flow, as long as it is safe to do so. I have a couple of horses that decide, for whatever reason, they don't want to go forward and so they start going backwards. I encourage them to keep on stepping backwards and when they want to stop going backwards I ask them to go further backwards at which point going forwards seems an easier option. (Can I just emphasise I would also question why they didn't want to go forward in the first place). This is a wonderful technique if you're feeling resistant, or angry or depressed. Instead of fighting the feeling, agree with it, give it permission.

For example, if you don't want to do your bookwork, amplify that feeling of resistance, shout: "I refuse to do my books," and write it down several times. I usually do this for about 10-15 minutes by which point I discover the real reason why I don't want to do them – I am too exhausted, too scared, too overstretched. When I really give vent to that feeling I can find out what is really going on for me.

When horses have disputes in the herd, they usually settle right away. Rarely do horses hang onto grudges, plot revenge or demand that their way is the right way. Their desire for harmony always overrides. Fighting attracts attention and a disunited herd dynamic endangers the whole.

Healing Power of Horses Principle 7

"Give up the reins of control
Before in your life, it takes its toll."
Wendyism

CHAPTER 8

You can lead a horse to water but you can't make them drink (Or you can lead a partner to relationship, But you can't make them commit)

I WAS WALKING DOWN A COUNTRY lane with my not so tall but definitely dark and handsome 35 year old partner. I remember asking: "How can I be with you for 30 years and it not seem like a day, yet the thought of 30 years in another form of relationship seems like a prison sentence?".

You see I was talking to my little Welsh Mountain pony, Tiggy, that I had been with since my 12th birthday. Up until then very few human romantic relationships had got past the 2-3 year mark. Commitment was not my strong point. As for the thought of marriage, well that was an even worse idea, or so I believed. I had no self-belief, self-worth or trust in myself to believe I could have a long term relationship.

Despite the many limiting beliefs I held about relationships

I used to moan that my partner John remained married to his ex-wife. He had left her a few years before we met. Ten years into the relationship and he still hadn't divorced her. I kept saying that he didn't want to commit to me but when it was suggested that maybe I was the one who didn't want to commit to him, I just laughed. "Of course I do," I used to reply indignantly.

Deeper exploration of what was really going on for me soon revealed that *I* was definitely the one afraid of commitment. It was easier to pin the fear on John rather than actually look within myself. As soon as I identified and worked on those fears something shifted in me. I was able to let go of my need for him to be willing to commit to me and focused instead on my own willingness to honestly and fully commit to him.

Chuck Spezzano has a wonderful expression that I have used over and over again in numerous situations and always when I have a dilemma:

> **"Just commit to the truth being shown to you.**
> **If it is not true it will fall away and what is true will come in."**

I let go of my need for John to commit and worked on my own ability to commit to him. However, I was convinced that by committing to him the relationship would fall away. Thankfully it didn't. Miraculously, while I was chatting about something completely different, out of the blue a proposal came from him!

The secret Tiggy had revealed was about giving. I was able to give 100% of myself to him and all the other horses I have had. Their happiness was my joy; their freedom was my freedom. Their health was my health. I had no expectations. I just allowed myself to receive whatever they were able to give, even if that was nothing.

Initially when I was with John I made the relationship all about me and my needs. I never got any peace, nor did he because I was always demanding that *my* needs be met. Of course they could never be met by somebody else, although I didn't know that at the time. When I received that HIT (Horse Inspired Thought), I was even thinking of splitting with John because he was failing to meet my needs.

It had never even occurred to me that actually he might have needs too. So, after receiving that HIT from Tiggy I changed my attitude to John and began to adopt some of the techniques I had used with my horses. I started thinking and caring about his needs and released my expectations for my own needs to be met by him. That's not to say I went into sacrifice or denial over my needs but ironically, as I gave from my heart to John, everything I originally demanded from him came naturally.

The exciting thing about this principle is that you can't lose. As Chuck Spezzano suggests, if you commit and ask for the truth to be shown then either the person, or situation reflects that commitment back or, if it is not true, they or the situation fall away in perfect right timing.

Over the years as a spiritual counsellor and HEART (Holistic Equine Assisted Relationship Transformation) coach, one of the most common subjects that has continued to come up is commitment.

Some of the fears and myths surrounding commitment are:

- It might be the wrong person. What if someone better comes along?

- I am afraid to commit for life. It feels like a jail sentence

- I will get bored of them or they will get bored of me

- I may lose my freedom and spontaneity

- I may have to give up on my dreams and needs

- If I give all my love I may get hurt

- What if it doesn't work out?

- We have different needs.

Inability to commit can indicate an immaturity in relationships and a lack of self-belief. The need to play the field or hedge one's bets comes to mind. The grass always appears greener. Another indication of an inability to commit is that you're not at peace with who you are. You still hold the belief that there is something or someone better. When you're able to love and accept yourself fully you don't need other people to give you a sense of worth in a relationship. This allows you to be in the relationship in a healthy way. When you come from your own inner strength and self-worth, you don't have the fear of a relationship going wrong and of you being left distraught. With your inner sense of security and strength you know that you can survive the event and move on.

I promise you, you will. It really isn't the end of the world. Love doesn't hurt when a relationship ends. It is the loss of the *need* and attachment to that person for your self-worth that is the actual pain you are feeling. Unconditional love sets everyone free.

When you love yourself, being with someone else is lovely but it's not the end of the world if you aren't. You have a sense of wholeness rather than 'holeness' that needs filling up by someone else. You are able to be both independent and dependent = interdependent.

When you approach a relationship without the conscious or unconscious need for the other person to be your meal ticket, emotional crutch or your excuse not to be on your own, you will find that you attract relationships that aren't dogged by need. Consequently, you become more attractive to the other partner. There is no greater gift than being with someone just because you want to be with them, to give love and affection. When you are able to come from this level of unconditional love, commitment is easy. There is no fear of a partner going off with another person.

When you reach a higher level of maturity in a relationship, there is a great desire to bring happiness to your partner without sacrificing your own needs. If they find that happiness in someone else there is an ease of release that doesn't involve causing one party to be the 'bad guy'. There is a mutual respect and desire for each person to be OK. There is no intention to hurt and while there may be sadness there is a poignancy to it that doesn't leave a sense of betrayal.

Case Study 21: Is breaking up hard to do?

I am reminded how Tijor and Tiger Lily, two stunning looking horses, coped with their break up.

Tiger Lily was on loan to me from the equestrian centre but sadly had become lame. She was becoming stressed, worrying that she might be asked to be ridden. (She didn't realise she was in a place where she could safely express this fear and for it be honoured). Consequently, her fear made her over-protective of herself and wary of anyone coming into her stable. I could see she was unhappy but didn't know what to do for the best.

The situation was further complicated by the fact that she had struck up an intense relationship and pair bond with Tijor. She and my ex show jumper Tijor went everywhere together in the field, grazed side-by-side and were often seen happily away from the main herd.

I agonised over what to do. I didn't want to send her back to her owner and break Tijor's heart. Nor did I want her to stay unhappy. However, her protective behaviour was increasing, so I said to her: "you need to give me a really clear sign as to what you want to do. If you want to go home to your owner you need to connect with her."

Unfortunately, I had changed phones and mislaid the owner's number. So you could have knocked me down with a feather, when, within a week or two of me having the conversation with

Tiger Lily, her owner walked in. You have to bear in mind I only used to see or hear from her once or twice a year.

I took it that Tiger Lily wanted to go home. Up until that day I had been worrying about how the two horses would cope being apart. My own pain from relationship splits in the past had been coming through. The day arrived and the horsebox pulled up. Tiger Lily marched into the box. I was holding up ok until Tijor and Tiger Lily whinnied to one another, a bit likes a scene between Heathcliff and Cathy in Wuthering Heights. That was it - one blubbering me!

After she left, I turned Tijor out into his field. Barclay walked up to him and gave him a nuzzle as if to say "you'll be alright mate" and Tijor strolled down the field with his head low and his stride slow.

After an excruciating night of endless mind chatter about whether I had done the right thing, feeling guilty for splitting them up and all the other self-attack, I went to the field to see how Tijor was doing. Lo and behold he was back with his earlier girlfriend Penny Black as if they had never been apart!

However it is worth noting that for some horses, losing their special human or pair bond horse, can be very traumatic and distressing, especially if they haven't been "told" what is going on.

I think what made it easier for these two horses was knowing what was going on and also putting Tiger Lily's happiness ahead of everything. This brought an authentic ending for all.

The biggest mistake that can be made regarding commitment is to make it all about you. While it is important to maintain a sense of self and one's own needs, commitment becomes easy when you consider your partner's needs and happiness as well as your own.

Case Study 22: It's a dog's life

While on holiday in Malta my dearly beloved hubby fell in love with a little stray dog and proceeded to make steps to bring her home. Meanwhile, having never had any experience of dogs, I had the opportunity, at exactly the same time, to take on a very distressed border collie, Bob, in the UK. If we were going to have one dog, we just might as well have two.

My observations of people with dogs in the neighbourhood were that they religiously took them for walks at 6a.m. and 11p.m. and presumably throughout the day. The mere thought of having to get up at the unearthly hour of 6a.m. filled me with dread but nonetheless I did my duty. Within a week I was a wreck, not only because of all the early mornings and late nights but also because the responsibility of owning a dog was huge in comparison to owning other animals. Horses take care of themselves most of the day in a field and cats come and go as they please.

I was so stressed out that I seriously contemplated having to reluctantly send him back. I was just deliberating making the phone call when I spotted Bob galloping as fast as his legs could carry him around one of the fields on the farm where I had my horses. I could feel the joy exuding from him as he freed himself from the fetters and chains he had spent most of his life tied to.

In that moment I heard a loud: 'this is about him not you'. When I realised that I was being given the opportunity to bring so much joy and freedom to this little dog's life I committed to him there and then. The amazing thing that happens when you commit to situations that seem impossible to figure out is that other possibilities suddenly appear.

When I really looked at our situation I realised that walking the dog at 6 a.m. and 11 p.m. wasn't a necessity. Yes, he needed a late night loo break which we had an ample size garden for but as for exercise he was one of the lucky dogs whose whole day involved running around the farm and herding the horses. We found a workable solution that met each other's needs entirely and we enjoyed a further easy 14 years together.

Awareness is power

Once I have greater awareness of why I am in a space, I am able to choose to do something about it – or not. The problems arise when I keep resisting the lesson or feeling.

We have a mare who finds it a bit difficult to bend in a certain direction. If you force her, she 'bananas up', i.e. flexes her body in the wrong direction. So, going round to the right she keeps bending to the left. When she bends in the wrong direction we turn her in that direction so that we have her in the correct bend. She usually bananas herself to the outside again but instead of fighting this we turn her towards the outside again. Although I may not immediately be getting the actual directional shapes I intended, I still achieve my ultimate aim.

Although we haven't got exactly what we wanted straight away, the key thing is that we haven't got into a fight with one another. I have still reached my goal and she has had her desires met. Interestingly, after a while the horse loosens up and the very thing I wanted in the first place, which was for her to go round in a circle, starts to happen.

Carrying through to consequence

I have known someone do something similar when their kid resisted going to bed. The child wanted to stay up, so the parent stayed up with the child and every time the child started getting a bit sleepy she would wake the child up. Eventually, the child insisted on going to bed. When morning came round she didn't let the child sleep in but got her up at normal time. She did this several nights in a row and soon the child stopped resisting going to bed in the first place.

> *"When you make it okay*
> *it will go away."*
> **Wendyism**

In spiritual terms it is often called the path of least resistance. If you think of a stream coming down the mountain, it will flow wherever it is not blocked. It doesn't necessarily mean it goes in a straight line. Often it meanders its way. As it meets an obstacle it changes direction or finds the easiest path through. I'm not saying this is the answer for every sort of relationship challenge but it is worth giving it a try to bring peace.

Sometimes it is easy to use a relationship issue as a disguise for your fear of moving towards your purpose.

Healing Power of Horses Principle 8

> *"Commit today*
> *To see if they stay.*
> *If they don't they're not for you.*
> *If it is true, one becomes two."*
> **Wendyism**

CHAPTER 9

It's no good flogging a dead horse
Is it time to commit or quit?

WHAT CREATES DEADNESS? IS THE relationship really dead?
 Knowing when to quit is possibly one of life's hardest challenges. It's not uncommon to blame yourself, your partner or boss if a relationship is not working or moving forward. 'There must be something wrong with me,' is often the annoying critical self-voice we hear when somebody won't commit. It is easy to go into the: 'me or thee must love more, do more, care more, stop winding him up, be more patient and understanding etc.' Or, have you ever continually excused somebody's behaviour, trying to make them right when everything deep down in you is screaming 'you should ******* let go?'

Unfortunately, these can be signs of very low self-esteem, lack of self-love and poor self-worth. "But I love him and I want to take care of him," I often hear as an excuse. Too often we live in the future fantasy of the relationship rather than facing the reality of what is happening.

Case Study 23: Distant relationship

"He just needs time to sort his life out," implored Pam.

I had been working with Pam for over a year and in that time she had only received a handful of texts and one visit from her supposed boyfriend, even though he was often in the area.

We had spent many a conversation looking at this 'relationship'.

"How can I make him love me and want to be with me?" she pleaded.

I suggested we went into the herd to see what answers came up.

As we went into the field one of the horses, Nemo, popped his head up. However, previous to this point we had already chosen another horse to represent her 'partner'. As we went over to Bea, who was busy eating hay, Nemo intercepted Pam.

Nemo is one of the most loving, gentle and generous horses you could ever wish to meet. Pam was very touched that he wanted to be with her. After greeting him we continued towards the other horse. Bea was still munching her hay and not acknowledging Pam in any way, shape or form.

We continued conversing about her distant 'relationship', specifically how she could get him to give her some acknowledgement. (Bea had *still* not looked up from her hay or acknowledged Pam).

"I just need to be patient and understanding, He has got a lot going on for him" she justified.

So I suggested she act that out with Bea. She patiently stood by Bea hoping she would understand that Pam wanted to be with her.

Bea carried on eating hay; despite the fact that Pam was close enough to touch her. Bea still didn't look up at her which is unusual when you're that close. Pam stood and waited, then stood some more and continued waiting. Pam began to realise the futility of waiting for this horse to acknowledge her.

I set about changing Pam's mind-set and energy. I invited her to affirm that she was loved, loving and lovable and that she deserved to have a healthy relationship. Bea continued to eat hay and then wandered off in another direction while Nemo, who was on the other side of the paddock, came marching over completely of his own volition, towards her.

Pam was overwhelmed and overjoyed that Nemo went out of his way to be with her.

"This is what a loving relationship looks like," I explained "they *want* to be with you! When you have self-belief and self-love you attract them to you."

The horses showed her more about the cold stark reality of her relationship in less than an hour than any amount of conversation or years of counselling she had done previously.

Maybe it's called long "distant" relationship for a reason!

Case Study 24: The importance of being Earnest

On another occasion we were at a horse sanctuary where I was training a group of students on my HEART Foundation Course for Equine Assisted Facilitators. One student had experienced a life dogged by abuse and a controlling partner.

We were doing an exercise on forgiveness and were working with an amazing horse called Ernie, a staggering 18h.h. shire horse. He had suffered horrendous abuse from a farmer, having been subjected to such pain from a human…..all for growing too big.

This physically and emotionally damaged horse had become so aggressive towards humans that he was extremely dangerous, to the extent that he had put several people in hospital. His days had been numbered when he was rescued by this amazing sanctuary called Mane Chance, where the work of James French and his Trust Technique enabled Ernie to enjoy humans again.

We walked out to the field where the herds were grazing and asked the horses for a volunteer. Incredibly, Ernie left his mates and strode towards us. I facilitated the forgiveness work I was doing with the students in a group surrounding Ernie in a horseshoe shape. I thought we had finished but Ernie continued to stand there at liberty loose with no head collar on him and I realised that there was still work to be done. I became inspired to work on forgiving the farmer, and even Ernie, for allowing the abuse to happen. This time when we completed the exercise I witnessed the most amazing scene ever. Ernie took his time and turned his head to acknowledge each and every one of us with a look of gratitude. He then strolled off back to his herd. We all fell in a sobbing heap, facilitators included, of extreme awe and profound amazement.

Coming back to the student with the abusive background, like a lot of us she had become addicted to her own story and up until that point never really moved on with her life. What was so poignant for her was the realisation that if this horse, even with his level of abuse, could let go of his story and return to being a truly loving, kind spirit, then what excuse did she have as a human to continue to hold onto her story and keep reliving it every time she told somebody about it?

Sadly, as most women in abusive situations know only too well, sometimes the fear of leaving can be greater than the fear of staying. Fear of the consequences: financial loss, losing the children, being lonely, feeling a failure, not wanting to admit defeat are all too often some of the reasons for staying. The painful reality is that the situation very rarely changes and it is knowing when to cut your losses and to start loving yourself enough to say: "I deserve better than this."

Since then, this student's life has now completely taken off with many miracles and manifestations regularly happening.

A personal anecdote. Forgiveness doesn't mean to condone.

My own life story involved a very abusive partner. The relationship had started as a bit of a whirlwind and I felt quite swept off my feet with compliments and gifts. However, after about a year and a heavy night of drinking the violence began.

As is often the case, the following day he was absolutely full of remorse. Of course I forgave him. I believed it was an accident. Unfortunately, a pattern had begun. He would get drunk, the violence would increase and the next day he would be full of remorse, especially when I said it was over. I fell for the begging and promises it would never happen again *every time*.

The only problem now was my partner started to make threats that, if I left him, my horses would suffer and so would I. Naturally that was my button pusher. I could just about cope with things happening to me but the thought that he might take his rage out on my horses was too much to bear.

In most domestic violence situations, involving police or the authorities can be like a red rag to a bull. Thankfully, I was divinely directed to dealing with the situation in a different way (see Chapter 2).

Although I continually forgave him, and always justifying myself staying in the situation by saying I loved him, I had to reach the point where love and respect for myself had to supersede at some point.

Deep in your soul you *know* the answer to a situation but sometimes you may want to go against your own advice. However, life never presents just one opportunity to get the right answer to all your challenges. Your inner teacher works with the decision you make in the moment and, if you're not ready to make the highest decision, it really doesn't matter. All paths lead home. You may go the scenic route and have a few cul de sacs thrown in but your authentic self will find its way out eventually.

Case Study 25: Unavailable, Unsuitable, Unwilling

I was running a retreat weekend and a very astute and intelligent lady was one of the participants, who came with the frustration that she couldn't get a partner to commit to her.

One of the exercises was to go around and choose a horse to work with. With about 30 to choose from this shouldn't have been too difficult a task. However, each horse she chose was unavailable for some reason, either it was lame, about to work in the riding centre or was privately owned. She tried six horses in all. (This seems to happen quite a lot with women on my courses).

Of the ones that were available, as she went up to them they ignored her or backed off from her. She eventually chose Lordi but as she attempted the exercises he just kept pulling her around and doing only what he wanted. I asked her to consider how this highlighted her relationship patterns and what she may be sending out as a script.

"I don't matter"

"My needs don't count"

"I am desperate for a partner"

These were just some of her scripts. When she got her HIT

(Horse Inspired Thought) from the horses she realised that most of the men she attracted were just like them: unsuitable, unavailable or lame ducks. When she did find someone she became so needy, her energy field was too repelling and off they went or she was so desperate to keep them she would sacrifice her integrity and needs and they would just do whatever they wanted with little regard to her.

Initially, she was rather overwhelmed when she realised that it was her own beliefs and energies that were the cause. However, rather than staying a victim she chose to turn those beliefs around and when she stopped being so needy and desperate she attracted a really lovely man.

What is interesting is that she had spent a fortune on counselling, therapy and traditional coaching with little change. The herd gave her the answer in one day. Through the horses acting as they did, she was able to claim back her power.

Realising that your beliefs co-create your reality can seem a bitter pill to swallow, but it does lead to considerable self-empowerment. Consider this: if you have managed to create a life like this unconsciously, imagine what your life could be like when you become conscious of and present to, your belief systems and choices. You have the power to change the direction of your life in an instant.

Healing Power of Horses Principle 9

"Release the need to know when and why
Just trust us to show you how to get by."
The horses

CHAPTER 10

Unbridled Passion
Do what you love,
love what you do

When I discuss passion in this Chapter I am not really referring to the intimate happenings between two people (although that is a likely by product in some cases), instead I am talking about an energy that fills your veins, like an electric charge running through the very centre of your being.

Few people fail to be moved by the wondrous sight of a herd of excited horses hurtling around, galloping together and feeling carefree. It is one of the few things that genuinely stirs me right to the core of my being, Even after over 40 years of being and working with horses. The sheer group mass of horse power is palpable.

Personal Anecdote: The ride of my life

I actually 'stole' my first ride, on a magnificent 15h.h. grey mare. I was out with friends and, as young kids do, I was egged on to mount this majestic creature. (Bear in mind that I didn't even have a bridle, saddle or any means to control the horse). I had never had a riding lesson or even sat on a horse before. Not quite in the British Horse Society's manual on how to ride!

Amazingly, this mare allowed me to clamber on her. She stood innocently and unsuspectingly as I climbed the fence she was standing by, my heart pounding with excitement, fear and blind stupidity. I grabbed a bit of her mane and gingerly slid my 9 year old legs over her back. This surprised steed galloped full pelt down the field with her fellow herd members. I can't quite remember whether I fell off, got off or was bucked off. I do though remember the adrenalin fuelled rush and the indescribable life force that circulated through my entire body.

I was hooked. Just how somebody I am guessing would feel when they had their first high from a drug. And so my addiction, or what I'd rather call my passion, for horses started.

I am really curious about what it is that horses offer me that not only keeps me sane (that's debatable) and on more than one occasion in my life, alive. As I think of my horses I am filled with awe. If they were taken away from me I would feel as though I'd lost my connection to the Great Organising Dynamic of life. There is a divinity deep within their essence that encourages me not to give up completely when challenges become overwhelming.

The passion I have for my horses and work allows me to feel so fulfilled that my cup runneth over with love and passion for my husband, John. He doesn't demand anything of me nor do

I of him. The strength of our partnership is there as a natural consequence of following my heart to do the things in life that are authentic for me.

Difficulties arise when you get caught up in the roles, responsibilities and routines of life and stop listening to your heart. Not that following your dreams and heart is without the occasional difficulty. Thankfully, as I remember saying to a friend who was always describing her life as a nightmare "at least you can wake up from nightmares." They do not have to be recurring. If they are, when following your heart and dreams, it usually means some form of change or new level of understanding and growth is needed.

Case Study 26: Depression to Elation

One group of young adults came for a day with the horses. One girl was extremely depressed, and at first was not interested in joining in the group activity. She had never had any experience with horses before. However as we progressed through the day working with different horses, her energy started to completely change.

Throughout the day her successes and insights with the horses slowly increased her confidence. By the end of the day she was really animated and her spirits had lifted quite considerably. The day inspired her so much that she asked if she could become a volunteer at the centre.

There then became an opportunity to start an apprenticeship at the centre. At the interview I asked one of my usual questions of why the job was important to her. I was taken aback by her unusual reply. "I need this job for my emotional wellbeing" she replied. With an answer like that the job was instantly hers.

Watching her transformation from being a miserable member of an HR team to a happy head groom working with passion and purpose has definitely been one of the best experiences for me as an employer I have ever had.

Often when we are afraid to move forward to follow our passion it is very easy to blame our partner, lack of money or some other external reason. This story helps to illustrate that.

Case Study 27: It is not your partner stopping you

One of my students was feeling very frustrated with her situation. Outwardly she had everything going for her: a committed husband, family business and great kids. However, she had spent years supporting her husband but really wanted to do something for herself but felt she couldn't.

Sam, the horse, started the exercise, heading towards the obstacle that represented her true passion. He came to a decisive halt and my student got really angry. "This is just what happens at home. I talk about what I want to do and my husband doesn't take me seriously and flatly refuses to entertain the idea. I just want to scream and run away." I suggested she did just that in the field!

She ran away, ranting and raving at the top of her voice. Within less than five minutes a truly remarkable thing happened. The lady was on the opposite side of the paddock, nowhere near the obstacle that represented her true passion, when Sam completely of his own volition strolled over to the obstacle and just stood there, waiting for her.

"What did that represent for you?" I enquired.

She replied that she realised her anger wasn't really about her husband. She discovered that, whilst she was feeling overwhelmed with all the business and home responsibilities, the anger and frustration was really covering up how afraid she was of doing what she really wanted to do. She had been using her husband as the perfect excuse for not moving forward to her true purpose and passion.

She also deduced from Sam's behaviour around the obstacle, that when she really got in touch with her emotions (especially the fear) and passion, Sam (representing her husband) supported her desires without any coercion. All she needed to do was find the courage within herself to take the next step towards her true passion and everything would fall in place.

So, what is it that lights up your soul with joy, calls your spirit and satiates your soul? Without a true passion there is a deadness within you that affects the stability of your relationships. When you have passion and enthusiasm, whether that is with a job, hobby or purpose, that energy is infectious. It brings others to life, it is inspiring and it is joyous.

When your own passion is thwarted, either through anger, miscommunication or life events, there is a danger that your relationships will be affected too. Have you ever been in a job that is really not for you and it seems as if everyone else is only there because they think they should be. They either want to please their parents or just want the money. They hold the belief that they can't do what they are passionate about **and** earn money? Would you agree that it is hell being in this type of environment?

Several people from the City, who have come on the Healing Power of Horses workshops at our centre, have felt the tranquillity, clean air and enjoyed being with the horses. The connection with nature has inspired some of them so much that they have been willing to give up their so-called security. They realised the stress and toll it was taking on their health was costing a much higher price than the wage they were receiving.

Sadly, so many people work in jobs they are not passionate about. They sell their soul for the money, status or security. The effect is that day-by-day another piece of them dies and when they feel dead and lifeless within, the chances are the key people in their life feel that deadness too.

In these situations, the temptation is to blame your deadness on things outside of you: the job, the boss, the family, the partner etc. Rather than admit that the deadness is due to your fear of taking a step towards your passion, people try to feel alive again and fill a void by having affairs and allowing relationships to break down.

When I look at my relationship with my horses, the first thing I notice is that I never get really angry with them. I might have a moment of frustration but that is only when I am usually being controlling or unclear. I usually have a mini tantrum and then my energy is clear. Nothing puts a dampener on passion more than unexpressed anger, especially in the bedroom department.

If your partner, boss or somebody else appears to be making you respond with anger (technically no-one can *make* you feel anything), then find a way to release that emotion. If it doesn't feel safe or appropriate to express that feeling to them personally, write it out, get your rage down on paper. You don't have to send the letter, in fact it's probably wise not to.

Take a moment to think of something that makes you angry and something you are passionate about. Can you feel that the physical energy of anger is the same as the physical energy of passion? If you suppress your anger, you cannot feel passion. It is one and the same energy.

Another thing that feeds my passion for the horses is their 'horsanilites'. I adore their little cheeky ways.

- Copper always let himself out of his stable when he decided it was time for him to go to the field. Not only would he let himself out, he used to go around letting the other horses out too.

- I was amazed at how clever Branston was. We used to come into work in the mornings to discover the horses were out on the bridle path. I was pretty positive that I had tied the gate the night before. It happened time and again, so we deduced it must be some kids playing a prank. We started coming in earlier to see if we could catch the culprit. If I hadn't seen it with my very own eyes, I would never have believed that two horses could work together to untie the rope round the gate with their teeth?

I am equally passionate about transforming the lives of horses and humans. Just as I feel excited when I see my herd galloping up the field, I become overjoyed when my clients make breakthroughs.

Ask yourself right now: what turns the light on behind your eyes? What makes your heart happy and your soul sing? Maybe it is something simple like being in nature, watching a stunning sunset. Daft as it may seem for a 50 plus adult, I always get excited when I see a rainbow and if it is a double or triple one I feel really thrilled. Could it be a song or piece of music that rouses, resonates and raises your passion?

Now imagine bringing that animated energy to a relationship that has felt a bit dead or dispassionate. With that fire in your belly can you feel how you would be able to light up and breathe life back into the partnership? What creates instability in a relationship is the demand for passion from the other person. The key to a stable relationship is finding that passion for yourself and then sharing your resulting energy.

Too often when we grow up we feel forced to follow parental guidance or have a need for them to be proud and approving. This usually results in us making a diverted turn. The greater the need for parental pride or approval, the more we are likely to stay on the wrong track, until our inner spirit can bear it no longer. The more teenagers I work with, the more I see this dilemma.

Case Study 28: Rosie, Riding and Wrists

One girl who came to see me had a real affinity with not just horses but all animals. Her heart, mind and soul really wanted her to go down the animal care route but her mother (possibly projecting her own fears and desires onto her) insisted that she wouldn't be able to earn much money in this field and forced her down the academic route. The young girl hated this with a passion. Learning like that was hell on earth for her and each week I noticed her energy getting weaker and her life force disappearing.

Talking with her mum resulted in more and more arguments and I felt this young girl's spirit just wanted to die. She couldn't express how angry she felt and being an extremely sensitive soul, this was highly dangerous to her health.

She was attracted to an equally sensitive mare of mine, Rosie, who had suffered a breakdown when she was in Ireland because she was pushed too hard to perform when younger. On this particular occasion, the teenager was riding her as normal but was secretly seething with anger about her school situation. Unfortunately, when you suppress your emotions, they can inadvertently be picked up by the horse. That is exactly what happened. My mare took flight and p****d off round the arena causing the teenager to lose her stirrup and fall, fracturing her wrist. It was a perfect reflection. She couldn't pretend any longer that she too was equally p****d off with her situation.

Ironically, her fractured right wrist gave her some borrowed time around her exam period. As she was unable to write, the pressure to perform was off her. She was given additional support and was able to cope with her exams better.

She hadn't woken up that Sunday morning and consciously thought: "I'll wind up Rosie today so I can fall off and break my wrist, then I can get out of the pressure of my exams."

However, her body, mind and soul conspired to create the perfect scenario to get her out of a situation.

I am reminded of another client where something very similar had happened.

Case Study 29: The truth will out itself

One lady had been working on increasing her confidence throughout the summer. She had regained her confidence and was happily riding her wonderful horse. Then, two days before she was due back to her job, she was riding around when her horse seemingly spooked (something he never normally did) and she fell, breaking several ribs.

I must confess that my first thought was: 'she's going to sue me.' Nevertheless, she continued our sessions from her hospital bed and it transpired that, deep down, she dreaded going back to her job she hated in a politically fraught atmosphere. Unconsciously, she *had* to create the perfect reason for not returning.

As I plumped up her pillows I asked her what she was really passionate about. It came to light she had always wanted to be a healer. Because she was off work for so long, waiting for her broken ribs to heal, she had the space to think about what she really wanted to do. When she was better she quit her job and became a qualified healer and fulfilled her passion.

It can be hard to believe that, in a split second, we make a conscious choice to allow something to happen. However, because we make the decision in a 'nano' moment, our mind buries that decision deep in our subconscious. Your unconscious and subconscious thoughts can then rule your life far more than your conscious thinking.

To reiterate, it is vitally important to find what creates passion in you. Sometimes, for the sake of your sanity you just have to let go of the logical voices in your head saying 'you can't possibly do that' or 'you can't afford to do this' and follow what is really in your heart.

Another of my real passions is writing, for my own pleasure, not necessarily for others to read. I had made a commitment to myself to get this book out publically. Like most of my projects I am first out of the starting gate but then I allow life and everything and everyone else's needs to takeover.

After reaching a very rare but all time low (because I realise now my spirit was not being fed with my writing passion), I began to feel as though I was dying inside. Even the horses that normally bring me joy and passion were not inspiring me. As has been my usual pattern of beating myself up for not completing yet another project, I felt I had reached the end of the road. I was in complete and utter despair.

Out of the blue I received a call from a wonderful trainer, Kate Gerry, who I had worked with once before. It came just as I was desperately asking the Divine for help. She insisted that I attended a retreat that she was organising; 'Creating Space and Joy for Business Owners'. I already had plans and certainly no money. I ummed and aahed. It was another major stretch financially. I couldn't really justify yet another course. I had so many other uses for the money, including bills to pay. I also felt guilty spending on myself, especially as John and I hadn't had a proper holiday because funds were low.

However, there was something deep in my soul telling me that I had to get there. So I ran it past John, checked I could alter the other plans without losing my investment, bit the bullet and even booked two extra days. Thankfully it was just what my soul needed. It gave me the space to follow my passion of writing. I finally finished this book.

An interesting aside is that, although I had been very anxious about the cost of the break, while I was on the course several people booked onto my courses, which more than paid for the cost of my retreat.

> *"When you follow your passion your heart opens,*
> *When your heart doors open wider,*
> *Other doors are able to open too in more ways than one."*
> *Wendyism*

The horses have given me so much, this book is also a way of giving back to them and of honouring the entire horse kingdom for the healing insights and wonderful life they have provided for me and so many of my clients.

Healing Power of Horses Principle 10

> *"Follow your passion to open your heart,*
> *And you will notice your life will restart."*
> *Wendyism*

CHAPTER 11

Loving Leadership
Finding your authentic place in the herd of life

Studying the natural behaviour of a herd of horses can provide everything you need to know about leadership. Horses have a code of practice that has kept them alive, safe, fed and able to reproduce for millions of years, in spite of being the tastiest prey animal.

So, what are their secrets? How can their code of behaviour help you with different relationships? How do you keep an organisation running smoothly? How do you maintain family harmony? How can you be a leader in a relationship without being the bossy controller? How do you create an equal partnership, yet still be a leader?

An interesting fact about horses is that most of them actually don't want the role of leader. It carries too much responsibility and the rewards are few. The leader is the horse on the edge of the herd and can be vulnerable to attack from predators. They have to defend the herd, suss out the terrain and be responsible for finding the next meal.

Horses are motivated to follow – but not just to follow any horse. They have to feel that the horse they are following will keep them safe and make appropriate decisions. The same applies to humans and their leaders.

Another fascinating fact is that a stable herd has different types of leaders, typically an alpha leader, a passive leader and a driver leader.

- Alpha leaders can be the bossy ones. They rule through aggression (not so common in wild herds) or assertion i.e. 'don't mess with me'. They are great at disciplining the herd and not allowing young whippersnapper horses to come up the ranks too quickly. In wild herds the alpha leader is nearly always a mare but in modern day herds the leader can be of either sex.

   At our hay stations in the field Midnight is the Alpha. She eats from whatever hay feeder she chooses. She doesn't have to say or do much, as the other horses pick up on her strong leadership energy and react accordingly without much discussion. What she says goes!

- The Passive leader is in a great position as he has the most influence. This horse doesn't need to broadcast its status and title. It makes decisions quietly, such as where and when to eat and drink. Interestingly, this is the horse other horses look to most for guidance. Typically this can be more of the lead horse than any of the others.

   Brock is our Passive leader. He can't be bothered with the politics of who wants to be leader because he knows the herd looks to him for important decisions. When the horses come in from the field and there is a new, scary looking obstacle, he typically says: "Oh for goodness sake. Just walk past it." The herd then follows him without hesitation.

- There is also the leader from behind, the Driver, who drives and directs the herd. In the wild, the stallion often takes this role but again in modern herds this can be any horse. This is almost like the Alpha but at the rear of the heard. This horse may not want a front leadership role but he/she still has influence. This can be a vulnerable position in the herd because a horse at the back can be plucked off by a pesky predator.

These leadership roles can change in an instant and the horse with the most knowledge about a situation e.g. where to get the best bit of grass, becomes the leader. The most important question they ask of any leader is "will your decision keep me safe?" Above all, safety is their number one priority. In the wild they do not have time to sit around in a meeting deciding whether they should go this way or that, they just get on with it.

No action = distraction = extermination

This is where working with horses can be so revealing. Most riders will agree that if you haven't made a decision within two seconds as to which direction you want to go in the horse will take over. As far as the horse is concerned, if you don't know where you want to go or what to do then the horse will decide for you. It is programmed to be decisive.

Case Study 30:
A little less conversation, a little more action

A wonderful friend of mine, who runs an on-line business, brought half a dozen or so of her staff to a team building and leadership day. The business was in its very early stages and the new team needed to find a way to establish clear and decisive work strategies. My co-equine coach, Jackie Davis, set them a task. They had 10 minutes to get a horse, Boris, from one end of the arena to the other without touching him.

After 10 minutes they were still talking about what to do. They hadn't been able to come to a decision on how they were going to complete the task because no one really wanted to take the lead. This reflected exactly what was happening in the organisation at the time: too much talk and not enough action.

We posed some coaching questions and the team members gradually began to organise themselves according to their strengths. The leadership roles sorted themselves out naturally and they all managed to get Boris to the other end of the arena. They took this learning back to the work place. The team became more productive and went on to achieve award-winning success.

Case Study 31: Going round and round in circles

On another occasion I was riding out with a business friend of mine, Elaine and her fellow director. We weren't *meant* to be having a therapeutic coaching session, just a 45 minute fun ride. However, horses are unable to discern if they should provide therapy or just a ride. All they do is respond to the energy they are receiving in that moment

Over an hour had passed and we weren't even a quarter of the way round. Tijor, out in front, just kept going round in circles and the other horse, Sam, refused to go anywhere, preferring to eat. I was piggy in the middle, trying to help both riders from my horse Rodney.

All three horses knew the route like the back of their hand. They knew the bits where we trotted or cantered and the places we just sauntered. We were on the part of the route where they were usually up for a good trot but we just weren't going anywhere.

I asked Elaine and her business partner at that time: "What is really going on between you two?" They looked sheepishly at me, slightly embarrassed that they hadn't been able to completely hide their underlying frustration at one another. They then admitted that they were both annoyed with one another because they couldn't agree which direction to take the business in. Both had different priorities and both wanted their way to be the right way for the business.

One director had been going round in circles about which direction to take and not actually taking any action. The other director wanted to adopt a completely different working style and not get caught up in the 'ought tos and shoulds'. She needed a different type of working week and in protest – remember that Sam had just wanted to eat had opted to do nothing but eat. In addition to these problems neither of them enjoyed doing the back office work which was taking a huge amount of their energy.

I listened to their individual needs and reflected these back to them. They began to realise that both ideas were fantastic and, instead of each director trying to make the other do it their way, they opted to consider both strategies. They also realised that they needed to get a third person in to do the administration, which was really at the core of the problem. Just as they came to their HIT (Horse Inspired Thought) realisation, their horses started to move forward and we promptly completed the ride.

How horses can teach us to learn the art of interdependence

Torvill and Dean, the finest ice skating champions in the world, provide the best example of interdependence that I can think of. They have a really equal partnership; neither could work as successfully independently. To me they are the epitome of interdependence. They both depend on one other and yet are able to be independent of one another. Yet for all their seamlessly synchronised steps and their choreography of perfect partnership and parity, one of them – usually Christopher has to take the leadership role, otherwise there would be no defined direction to go in.

I believe this is fundamental in creating a stable relationship. It doesn't have to be yourself all the time; however one of you does need to take the lead. I believe I have an amazing equal partnership with my fabulous husband, John. When it comes to business, I slide into the leadership role and when it comes to our home life John tends to make the decisions. We move in and out of the leadership position within our relationship according to who has the best knowledge, confidence or vision in that moment. This is exactly what tends to happen in a stable herd.

Someone has to have the casting vote on what to eat, where to go, what to do, how to proceed etc. Teams, businesses and partnerships that abdicate this important responsibility will get stuck. Their colleagues just revert to their default way of working (or not). They will be like the rider whose horse takes over because they failed to make a clear decision within two seconds. Life events or situations will be forced upon them that they didn't really want and they will end up going in a direction they hadn't planned. Consider adopting the strategy horses use to keep your team alive by having different leadership positions.

Horses feel secure in the herd because they *all* have an important part to play. Each horse knows its place in the herd. Even the omega horse (bottom of the herd) has an essential role, as it absorbs all the anxieties and minimizes the stress from the rest of the herd. Everyone knows their place, their role and who they are meant to follow. This creates stability and security. Working with horses can really hone your leadership skills and help you to understand the position in which you feel most powerful and comfortable. They can show you how to be the authentic leader in your life.

Exercise 8: Lead the way

How can you become the leader that horses and people want to follow?

Ask yourself these 12 questions on leadership in your relationship, work, family and even yourself.

Am I leading myself with my own integrity and values or am I just following like a sheep for an easy life?

Am I leading by example and walking my talking or do I spout one thing and do the complete opposite?

Do I lead with empathy, love and understanding, or do I enjoy being stubborn and righteous?

Do I lead the way in forgiveness and letting go of grievances or am I holding on to grudges?

Do I lead the way in communication and connection or do I want to stay separate and sulk?

Do I lead the way in healing emotions and feelings or is it more important to make an idol of my pain that I can pay regular homage to?

Can I lead the way to happiness and fulfilment or do I play the victim?

Can I lead the way to peace and harmony or do I want to stay angry and right?

Can I lead the way to living my purpose or do I blame my fear of taking the next step on everyone else?

Dare I lead the way to authenticity or do I want to stay hiding behind my self-imposed roles and duties?

Dare I lead the way with unconditional love and compassion or stay in judgement criticism and attack?

Dare I lead the way in honesty and integrity or be like so many others and keep living a lie?

There are masses of really good books that provide advice about how to be a great leader, plus information on the pitfalls to avoid. However, none can equal the experiential learning that most horses have to offer. When horses are allowed to live authentically, they can reveal just who really is the boss!

Healing Power of Horses Principle 11

"Whatever you want your reality to be,
Find the way to take the lead
Become the leader others want to follow
Then your life and relationships will succeed."
Wendyism

CHAPTER 12

Stride to Success
The Spiritual Purpose of Relationships

MANY SPIRITUAL TEACHERS BELIEVE THAT everything you need to learn about life, love and the Universe comes to you through relationships, whether that relationship is with other people, yourself or the environment. There is nowhere you can be that you're not in a relationship, even with things like food, money and possessions. Each and every one of these relationships reflects an aspect of you, your emotions and your mind-set. Even the collective consciousness of humanity is reflected on the world stage. We are all one. Wherever you go, there you are.

Once you have an understanding of the powerful principles of harmonious herd life, I believe you have a recipe for relationships that can flourish through connection. Horses have survived successfully due to a strict code of communication, an ingrained need to create and maintain harmony and a desire for unity within the herd. Imagine how different the outer world would be if we all had this awareness.

When you come into this world you are perfect, whole and complete. However, your experiences and ancestral patterns, beliefs and unhealed emotions cause you to believe that you are otherwise. It is as if you hive parts of yourself off. Events happen in childhood and your interpretation of them usually makes you close down and shut the door to things like love, happiness, worthiness, etc. Your mission, should you wish to take it, is to reclaim these perceived missing parts.

Everyone you meet is a reflection of a part of you

As we discussed in Chapter 2 the people we meet reflect the parts of us that we either love or hate and show us where we are out of balance and what we believe about life. Unfortunately, it is difficult to see how people are trying to help us grow spiritually because we take things so personally.

By working with the horses you can get an even clearer picture of how authentic you are with your thoughts, feelings and desires in relationships. The horses offer an opportunity to discover how and where you hold yourself. They help break down the barriers and walls you have built. They help you discover your obstacles, blocked emotions and coping skills that are past their sell-by date. They show you where you have too much need for control and where you should strengthen your boundaries. They become your spiritual gurus. All without a word spoken.

All your relationships offer an opportunity for further healing. They show you where and what you believe to be unlovable about yourself. Sadly, many people grow up with the inherent belief that they are not good enough. It is one of the reasons why people fear intimacy and connection, believing that if their partner, friend or work colleague discovered a part that is not perfect enough, successful enough, clever enough, tall enough, thin enough, etc. then they would be rejected.

One of the biggest blocks to people coming on the workshops is their fear of exposure. We have become so clever (or so we think) at hiding what is really going on for us. For me this means we are giving our power away. Knowledge is power. Awareness is liberating and the Truth sets us free.

Heaven is entered two by two

Heaven, whatever that means to you for the sake of simplicity let's take it to be a place of happiness, wholeness and oneness is reached when you have balanced your masculine and feminine energies, integrated your 'good' and your 'bad' and let go of your erroneous beliefs in separation.

We don't have to wait until we die, hoping we have accrued enough brownie points to be 'in heaven'. Heaven can be right now, a state of being. Being happy, being harmony, being love.

Life is just, not fair

The main challenge in life is that it always responds to our beliefs, thoughts and assumptions. As we discussed in Chapter 1, what we are experiencing in life is exactly what we are believing and no amount of temper tantrums can change this. (I have researched this fully!).

Whatever state you are in, you exude an energy that permeates everything and everyone around you.

Many people have given up on me through my life. I can be very frustrating.

I am not very controllable and tend to be a bit of a rebel and non-conformist. I am particularly bad at being told what to do. Ask me to do something and there is a 99.9% chance that I'll say yes. Tell me what to do and I can guarantee 100% that I won't do it. I am so like a couple of my horses, Boris and Harry.

My biggest challenge throughout life has often been that, as a pioneer in a lot of things, I've been a bit ahead of my time, which to others has made me seem quite radical. It has certainly put some people off in my field of influence, notably those who like conformity and things to stay as they are. I embrace change, recognising that without change there is no growth.

NO CHANGE = NO GROWTH

Fear of change comes from not having a basic trust in life, yourself or other people. Hence the need for everything to stay the same. It is so unrealistic though, not to mention boring!

Imagine if you stayed as a baby, you would be pretty big crawling around 30 years later.

Can you envisage if our seasons didn't change? An apple tree, for example, would be perpetually blossoming and not able to bear fruit. Or, if it was producing fruit, the fruit would over ripen and get ruined. Or, if it stayed in its winter state there would be no rejuvenation.

Case Study 32: Out of Balance

I normally embrace change and positively accept the new, so I was somewhat floored by such a deep and overwhelming attack and boy was it an attack, of negativity, depression and fear earlier in the year. It was paralysing, frightening and bewildering.

I knew something was afoot when even some of my own normally placid and trustworthy horses kicked me, another bit me and a couple of them put their ears back when I came near them. They told me, in no uncertain terms, that my energy field was way off kilter. My earlier experiences of dysfunctional relationships reminded me that if I was attracting this level of attack from outside I must be under attack inwardly. I also recognised that, because my business was not experiencing the success and flow it normally did, something was out of balance.

I have come to the conclusion that when your life gets turned upside down, and whatever you do fails to work, it usually means it's time for a shift in consciousness.

I had been going through an intense internal period of feeling unwanted and unlovable, a pattern of belief I discovered I had been carrying since my time in the womb. The out-picturing in my life was that every direction I wanted to go in was blocked. 'Follow your dreams' all the modern sages would advise. I was trying to but far from being a dream my life was fast becoming a nightmare.

During this quantum growth period, I compensated for feeling unwanted by creating the exact opposite. I set up an excessive need for being wanted, by my animals and the people in my life. However, no matter how much your need may be met in the present, it can never compensate for the loss or need you had as a child. For example, if you needed £5 to buy food yesterday but you didn't have it so were left hungry, having £1,000,000 today can't undo the hunger you experienced then. That is why trying to get the needs of the past met in your current relationships is never successful.

Although initially I was really upset at how my horses were reacting to my energy field it saved me money in therapy. My experience with them was so much more profound and it prompted me to seek help.

Whatever type of relationship you are in, lessons will come up frequently, as you are invited to go to the next level of learning. That level might be a deeper connection, clearer communication, a greater level of intimacy or help with healing an old concept or belief. Life is always encouraging you to find the Truth in spite of the temptation to believe in appearances.

Since the age of 12 and inadvertently starting my collection of horses, I had developed a pattern of attracting more and more horses. Other than when I set up my first riding school and actively sought a few horses, nearly all the horses I have had the pleasure of meeting, and being custodian of, have come to me because they have been disowned or unwanted in some way. A few of them had experienced different levels of abuse as well.

Some of the horses had been unwanted because they wouldn't perform 'correctly', or behave well. They had been discarded because their inner frustration at humans caused them to be bad tempered, behave viciously or with resistance. Some of them had even been judged difficult, a potential killer or useless. Yet when they came to me, my natural love for animals and horses made it really easy for me to see beyond their behaviour to their true essence and to love them unconditionally.

Case Study 33:
The good the bad and the not so ugly

On a retreat workshop that I was running, two of the ladies kept choosing the good looking horses that were more than a handful to deal with. Rosie, Harry and Smartie hadn't had a brilliant start to life and their treatment by humans had made them very fearful, causing them to be aggressive and defensive.

As we explored this behavioural pattern in them and what it might be reflecting, both ladies had their HITs (Horse Inspired Thoughts). They realised simultaneously that their choice of horses mirrored exactly their choice in men. They always went for the good looking, bad boys.

As the day progressed, they began to realise that they were attracting men who treated them as these women were inwardly treating themselves. Previously, they'd had no idea that the reason why they kept attracting these types of men was connected to their hidden thoughts and beliefs. They just thought they had been unlucky.

Having this pattern brought to their awareness allowed them to be far more conscious of choice of relationship.

It wasn't until I was in a relationship with a physically abusive partner that I began to change my life. Until that point I hadn't noticed that all my relationships had been abusive in some way. Things had become so bad I was compelled to find answers. Initially, I thought it was my responsibility to try to find a way to stop him drinking, a habit which tended to fuel the abuse. I remember phoning Al-Anon and being told that I was the one who needed to go into their 12 step programme. "But I'm not the one with the problem," I declared in a huff. Or so I thought.....

Despite being initially affronted by their suggestion, something deep within compelled me to attend an Al-Anon 12 step meeting. This was a turning point in my life that led me to the wonderful Louise Hay book *You Can Heal Your Life*. Both gave me the courage to change my circumstances by changing my thoughts, by healing my emotions and loving my disowned selves that my partner was out-picturing. Having discovered that somebody like my violent partner was merely my mirror, made me realise that I had some serious self-loving to do.

My job wasn't to change him, stop him drinking or to prevent him from acting violently. The purpose of the relationship was for me to increase my own level of self-worth and self-esteem to be able to set a boundary that said: "if you choose to carry on that behaviour that's your choice but it can't be towards me anymore." It wasn't said as a threat: "if you hit me again I will leave you," it was said with compassion and a new found love for myself. Ultimately, he had to take responsibilities for his choices, as I did for mine. Sadly, his illness of alcoholism stopped him from being able to control his violence and one day I just managed to believe in myself enough to say it was over. I had to realise that even though I loved him as well, it didn't mean I had to stay with him. Loving myself was more important.

After two years of really working on changing my beliefs and healing my emotions I managed to find the most wonderful partner who then became my husband. I am still very happily in love with him, even after more than 20 years together!

All the actions and reactions from the people in your life are secretly helping you to heal. These people may not be consciously aware of what they are doing but it is happening all the time, even in business.

I discovered this truth through my own business. For a while, I kept attracting livery customers (people who would pay me to look after their horses) who would just go without giving me the required one month's notice. Besides being left in the lurch financially, I could never really understand why I became so hurt emotionally. This happened over and over again.

One day, after such an incident, I was sitting silently in the field with my herd of horses, nursing my emotional pain at having been hurt again when the answer came to me. My father had suddenly left when I was young, without giving notice or informing me that he was leaving mum. He was in the navy in my earlier years, so periods of absence were normal. It was two years after he had left that I found out he wasn't coming back. Sadly, he hadn't even bothered to send Christmas or birthday cards to me. I didn't have a clue that this event had affected me so deeply until my livery customers kept leaving without notice – 30 years on.

Their actions helped me to grow spiritually. Their behaviour became a benefit for me, even though it took me several years to get this lesson. They say teachers are the slowest learners! Interestingly, since integrating, forgiving and healing that childhood trauma, I have rarely attracted 'disappearing' livery customers. As your beliefs, feelings and patterns with the different human relationships heal and improve; you are then invited to heal your relationship with the Divine, Life, God or the Universe –whatever the 'Allness' of life means to you.

Often we project so much of our parental stuff onto the 'Almighty'. It is most likely that if you had a strict, punitive father you probably see the Universe as a punishing and unfair place to be. If you grew up in a loving nurturing family environment, then you probably see the world as loving and nurturing.

Everyone you meet is there to help you grow and unfold

your true nature. When you realise this, you suddenly start to see that what is happening *to* you is not personal (people have no choice but to respond to your energy field) and yet it is happening personally *for* you.

At the end of the day relationships are simple. Everyone just wants love and acceptance for who they are. When you are able to give yourself unconditional love for every aspect of yourself you will find it easy to love and accept everybody else.

Remember everyone you meet is a part of you

Compassion, kindness and communication is at the Heart of Stable Relationships.

> *"Teach only love for that is all there is "*
> Course In Miracles

The Healing Power of Horses Principle 12

"Horses carry the wisdom of healing in their heart.

They offer it to any humans who possess the courage and humility to listen.

Are you ready for the "ride" of your life?"

Wendy Felicity Firmin-Price

If so, go straight to www.theheartofstablerelaionships.com/bonus5 for your free consultation booking code and let us have a conversation to see how the healing power of my horses can help you discover the HEART of stable relationships.

Thank you.
Wendy Felicity Firmin-Price